Marvin Ventrell has made a profound contribution to the field of child welfare law with this succinct and practical book. It really should be required reading for all lawyers appearing in child welfare court. It is an artful blending of the essentials of trial advocacy with the particulars of child welfare court. This book will empower attorneys to provide improved advocacy for children, parents, and agencies . . . and that, in turn, will lead to better judicial outcomes for our most vulnerable children and their families.

> *Jennifer L. Renne, Esq.*
> *Director, National Child Welfare Resource Center*
> *American Bar Association Center on Children and the Law*
> *Washington, DC*

Marvin Ventrell always starts his analysis at the right place: children's cases merit the same standards of excellence as do any other cases. In this book, he incorporates the best of traditional trial theory and practice to create a comprehensive "how to" manual for lawyers trying cases involving children and families. This book will benefit all lawyers, from novices to experienced litigators.

> *Richard Cozzola, Esq.*
> *Supervisory Attorney*
> *Children's Law Project, Legal Assistance Foundation of Metropolitan Chicago*
> *Chicago, Illinois*

Children and families deserve the best that advocates have to offer—and no one knows better than Marvin Ventrell how to teach those advocates how to practice their craft. This book conveys meaningful and practical knowledge on how to effectively represent clients who are often the most vulnerable people in the courtroom. I've had the honor of teaching with Mr. Ventrell for many years; this book sets out on the printed page the knowledge and passion that he conveys in person. It's a masterpiece on the art of child advocacy by a master of the art.

> *Hon. Robert McGahey*
> *District Court Trial Judge, Denver County*
> *Denver, Colorado*

TRIAL ADVOCACY FOR THE CHILD WELFARE LAWYER

TELLING THE STORY OF THE FAMILY

Trial Advocacy for the Child Welfare Lawyer

Telling the Story of the Family

Marvin Ventrell
Executive Director
Juvenile Law Society

National Institute for Trial Advocacy

Address inquiries to:

Reprint Permission
National Institute for Trial Advocacy
1685 38th Street, Suite 200
Boulder, CO 80301-2735
Phone: (800) 225-6482
Fax: (720) 890-7069
E-mail: permissions@nita.org

ISBN: 978-1-60156-149-7
FBA: 1149

Library of Congress Cataloging-in-Publication Data

Ventrell, Marvin R., 1959-
Trial advocacy for the child welfare lawyer: telling the story of the family / Marvin Ventrell.
    p. cm.
Includes index.
ISBN 978-1-60156-149-7
1. Child abuse--Law and legislation--United States--Trial practice. 2. Custody of children--United States--Trial practice. 3. Children--Legal status, laws, etc.--United States--Trial practice. I. Title.
  KF8925.C45V46 2011
  344.7303'27--dc22
                           2011009344

Printed in the United States of America

DEDICATION

To the trial competition students, faculty, and coaches of Regis Jesuit, St. Mary's Academy, Colorado Academy, and Aurora Central; and especially for Camille, Pat, and Lily.

CONTENTS

Contents

FOREWORD

Michael J. Dale[1]

Trying a child welfare case is difficult and complex work, about which there is little instruction in our literature. This book, *Trial Advocacy for the Child Welfare Lawyer: Telling the Story of the Family*, fills a critical and, until now, unmet need by providing clear, concise, and well-supported instruction for the child welfare trial lawyer.

Child welfare cases require an intimate knowledge of federal and state child welfare law as well as knowledge of the cross-professional disciplines of medicine, mental health, education, social work, and cultural competence. Child welfare cases are also highly emotionally charged, centering on personal and private family matters. Marvin Ventrell's practitioner's guide presents all of the central topics necessary to effectively try an abuse, neglect, and termination of parental rights case, and does so for each of the lawyers who participates: the prosecuting/agency lawyer, the parent's lawyer, and the child's lawyer.

The special contribution of this work is its guidance through each part of the trial using child welfare case specific illustrations. Litigating child welfare cases requires both generic trial skills and special skills unique to this field. This book blends the traditional art of trial advocacy and the niche art of child welfare advocacy.

Child welfare cases are typically tried within limited time frames. Lawyers must present opening statements and closing arguments that are brief, but also complete, clear, and persuasive. This book provides a method to do so.

Witness credibility is central to the child welfare case. A court's assessment of credibility frequently determines whether abuse or neglect is found and which placement is in a child's best interests. Because the credibility of fact and expert witnesses is so important, the proper execution of direct and cross-examinations is

---

1. Michael J. Dale is a Professor of Law at Nova Southeastern University Law Center in Fort Lauderdale, Florida. He teaches courses in trial advocacy, family law, juvenile law, civil procedure, conflict of laws, evidence, judicial administration, and international litigation. Before joining the Nova faculty, Professor Dale was in private practice and was Executive Director of the Youth Law Center in San Francisco, after serving as Attorney in Charge of the Special Litigation Unit of the Juvenile Rights Division of the Legal Aid Society of the City of New York. Professor Dale is a trial skills instructor for the National Institute for Trial Advocacy. He is the author of over seventy articles focusing primarily on juvenile and children's law topics. He is the author of *Representing the Child Client* published by Matthew Bender Co.

essential. The methods for witness examination presented here guide the lawyer in presenting clear and credible witness testimony.

The admission of exhibits, including school, agency, and medical records, photographs, other documents and tangible objects, all unique to the abuse and neglect process, requires a facility with trial evidence law and exhibit management. These skills are well taught in this book.

Personalizing one's client and establishing the unique importance of each case are also essential to success in this field. This is especially true where judges, as the finders of fact, sit exclusively in specialized child welfare courts and hear large numbers of similar sounding cases. This book provides a method for establishing the unique importance of each case through the use of trial storytelling. By viewing each child welfare trial as an opportunity to tell *The Story of the Family*, the lawyer can personalize each client and each case.

Trial Advocacy for the Child Welfare Lawyer is based on the author's extensive career as a trial lawyer in civil, criminal, juvenile delinquency, and child welfare court. The book also draws on Mr. Ventrell's work as a child welfare association director, a teacher, a trial teams coach, and a trial practice instructor. The text reflects Mr. Ventrell's long involvement with the National Institute for Trial Advocacy (NITA) and particularly the development of NITA's Rocky Mountain Child Advocacy Training Institute, where instructors employ many of the techniques discussed in this book. I am confident you will enjoy this readable, understandable, practical, and usable text that will advance the trial skills of all lawyers in this highly important, often misunderstood, and intensely personal area of the law.

PREFACE

THE ART OF TRIAL ADVOCACY

Informality is a precarious condition in a court process. Referencing the informal nature of the early juvenile courts, Justice Fortas of the U.S. Supreme Court wrote:

> Accordingly, the highest motives and most enlightened impulses led to a peculiar system for juveniles, unknown to our law . . . . Juvenile Court history has again demonstrated that unbridled discretion, however benevolently motivated, is frequently a poor substitute for principle and procedure.[1]

> There is evidence that [in an informal juvenile court] . . . the child receives the worst of both worlds; that he gets neither the protections accorded to adults nor the solicitous care . . . postulated for children.[2]

This language is part of the landmark ruling from the *Gault* case of 1967, in which the Supreme Court of the United States revolutionized the juvenile delinquency court from an informal "kiddie court" to a formalized due-process-based constitutional court. History teaches that formality of process is an indispensable component of justice.

Less than a decade later, an infrequently used component of the juvenile court, the child welfare function, would explode into use. As a result of newfound awareness of child abuse,[3] Congress passed the Child Abuse Prevention and Treatment Act in 1974.[4] This, in turn, led to a dramatic influx of child abuse cases under the juvenile court's child abuse jurisdiction.

The *Gault* decision, however, did not apply to the juvenile court's child welfare component, and so juvenile child welfare court would operate, as had the early juvenile delinquency court, in an informal fashion. This informality would take the form of courts without record, in-chambers proceedings, hearings without notice

---

1. In re Gault, 387 U.S. 1, 17 (1967).
2. *Gault* at 18.
3. Early awareness of the magnitude of child abuse in America led to the belief in the early 1960s that there were thousands of abused and neglected children. Data collected in the 1990s revealed approximately 3 million annual reports of child maltreatment involving approximately 5 million children each year. These reports led to approximately 1 million "founded" cases each year.
4. 42 U.S.C. § 5101.

and opportunity to be heard, ignorance of evidentiary standards, and what some commentators would later call *relaxed advocacy.*[5]

Relaxed advocacy can be described as a failure to adhere to the principles and procedures of zealous client representation. Rather than aggressively pursuing a client's interests, a relaxed advocate might choose, for example, to accept objectionable evidence on the theory that the court should hear *all* the information in order to make a "well-informed" decision as to a child's best interests. The problem with such an approach is that it operates counter to an advocacy-based system wherein justice is a by-product of competing interests. It takes the advocate out of the advocacy role and distorts, rather than promotes, the client's interests.

Yet such has been the culture of the child welfare court. And the art of trial advocacy was one of the casualties of this culture. Many court systems dispensed with opening and closing statements. Jury trials were authorized in a minority of jurisdictions and infrequently demanded even where they were authorized.[6] Leading questions were tolerated on direct examination, and unreliable evidence was entered into the record without objection. Witness exams were abbreviated to save time, and testimony was admitted by "offer of proof" without calling the witness or providing for cross-examination. While these breaches of the duty of zealous advocacy were not present in every court, they were widespread. Some of the more egregious violations occurred with children's counsel who failed to meet their clients or discover their clients' interests at all.[7] Rather than serve children and families, these practices disrespected, devalued, and disserved them.

This informal culture has not disappeared, but our child welfare courts are evolving. The lesson of *Gault* is now being applied in child welfare court proceedings. The federal government has implemented court evaluation programs that result in court improvement projects.[8] Private advocacy groups have achieved important policy improvements and implemented attorney education and training

---

5. Yale Child Advocacy Law Professor Jean Koh Peters used this term in her writings in the 1990s to describe lawyers' failure to engage in zealous advocacy.

6. Jury trials remain the exception in child welfare cases. A minority of jurisdictions, including Colorado, Michigan, Missouri, Texas, Wisconsin, and Wyoming, allow for jury trials (usually in the adjudication and/or termination phases). Advocates have reported to the Juvenile Law Society that even where authorized, jury cases are rare. www.juvenilelawsociety.org. Jury voir dire is not covered in this publication. For a discussion of jury voir dire generally, see STEVEN LUBET, MODERN TRIAL ADVOCACY: ANALYSIS AND PRACTICE, 4th Edition, NITA (2009).

7. ABA Presidential Working Group on the Unmet Legal Needs of Children and Their Families, America's Children at Risk: A National Agenda for Legal Action (1993).

8. http://www.acf.hhs.gov/programs/cb/.

programs.[9] Impact litigation has been used to reform court systems, and one federal district court held that a child's right to due process of law is violated when the child is not provided with competent independent legal counsel.[10] There is wider acceptance of the value of zealous advocacy in our child welfare courts now than ever before. As a result, the door in child welfare court has opened up to allow in the art of trial advocacy.

The essence of trial advocacy is *persuasion*. The role of the trial lawyer is to persuade the finder of fact within the context of the various parts of the trial. And nothing about that is inconsistent with the purposes and practices of the child welfare court.

So the time for this book has arrived, and I am privileged to write it. It represents my respect for the art of trial advocacy and my passion for the child and the family. It is the product of what I have been taught and what I believe.

Child welfare lawyers are trial lawyers. Every trial lawyer has a passionate, persuasive, and unique voice. Our calling as trial lawyers is to discover, respect, and deliver that voice. I believe it is our duty and our privilege to do so for children and families.

Marvin Ventrell
Denver, Colorado
February 2011

---

9. The National Institute for Trial Advocacy conducted the first Rocky Mountain Child Advocacy Training Institute in 1995; it is now in its sixteenth year. See also the programs of the ABA Center on Children and the Law and the National Association of Counsel for Children.
10. Kenny A. v. Perdue, 532 F.3d 1209, 1214 (11th Cir. 2006).

ACKNOWLEDGMENTS

Trial advocacy is an art passed from mentor to protégé through the generations. I am grateful to the many lawyers who gave freely to me their wisdom and experience. I am also grateful to the National Institute for Trial Advocacy (NITA) for serving as a fulcrum for the dissemination of this knowledge.

Special thanks are owed to NITA Program Director Mark Caldwell for accepting an invitation from a group of child advocates in 1994 to discuss the novel concept of a trial skills training for child welfare court lawyers. It worked, Mark.

It is not possible to acknowledge the hundreds of lawyers who have collaborated over the years to develop the methodology and techniques for teaching trial skills. It is imperative, however, that I acknowledge that I have done nothing more here than listen, learn, and pass it on.

CHAPTER ONE

CASE ANALYSIS
TELLING THE STORY OF THE FAMILY

Once upon a time . . . .[1]

> ### Take-Away
> *Theory + Theme = Case Story + Law = Outcome*

Case analysis begins before we are aware we are engaged in it. When a lawyer reviews a file for the first time, or hears a client explain a matter, the lawyer instinctively begins to apply the facts to the law and anticipate an outcome. That is what lawyers do. That is case analysis.

We performed case analysis as law students when we answered an exam question. We were given a fact pattern and asked to apply it to the law we had learned and describe the outcome. In its simplest form, case analysis is a formula:

Facts + Law = Outcome

Before we ever ask a question in court, therefore, we have at least intuitively determined that the fact we elicit, when applied to the law, will promote our client's position.

Intuition, however, will only get us so far. Trials are complicated, and child welfare proceedings are particularly so. They involve numerous and conflicting facts; they are coupled with complex law and procedure; and they occur within emotionally charged social, cultural, and family dynamics. It is the lawyer's job to package all of that complexity into a persuasive framework of the facts and law called the *Story of the Case*. Case analysis is the process of preparing the story of the case.

Once completed, the case analysis process and the resulting product—the story of the case—will guide each step of the presentation of the case and make the lawyer's job manageable. This is not exaggeration. Our story of the case guides us through

---

1. According to Wikipedia, "Once upon a time" is a stock phrase that has been used in some form since at least 1380 (according to the Oxford English Dictionary) in storytelling in the English language, and seems to have become a widely accepted convention for opening oral narratives by around 1600.

every moment of the trial: opening, direct examination, cross-examination, exhibits, objections, and closing. In each instance, we include or exclude, we promote or we refute, and we argue or we accept information as it serves our story of the case.

The Story of the Family

Storytelling is the art of portraying events through words and images. We like stories. We became accustomed to hearing them as children. We particularly like stories that are interesting and understandable; and when they are, we listen and become invested in the outcome. It is unrealistic to expect otherwise. No judge or juror should be relied on to take a disorganized set of facts, sort them out, and reach a conclusion. Yet that is what lawyers demand when we present a case without a story. It is the lawyer's job to do the heavy lifting, the sorting, sequencing, and delivering of the case in the form of a story.

Each case is a story, and the case analysis process allows us to prepare that story for persuasive storytelling. In child welfare cases, the story of the case is *The Story of the Family*. Every child welfare case is the story of a family told from either the perspective of the child, the parents, the extended family, the foster parents, or the department.

Storytelling and Bench Trials

The significant majority of child welfare cases are not tried before juries, but rather before a presiding judge, who also sits as the finder of fact (a bench trial).[2] This has led to the erroneous assumption that the art of trial advocacy and thematic storytelling are less appropriate or useful in child welfare cases. There is an absence of evidence that this is true.

Judges are people, too, and there is no evidence that they process information differently than lay people. Judges were children once and grew up hearing and being compelled by stories. It is a mistake and an abrogation of duty to assume that the judge will "sort it all out" without the benefit of persuasive packaging in the form of the case as a story.

This view is supported by new research that reveals that judges process information at trial more alike than unlike jurors. A significant majority of judges surveyed—78 percent—wanted lawyers to simplify technical issues. Moreover, 76

---

2. Jury trials are the exception in child welfare cases. A minority of jurisdictions, including Colorado, Michigan, Missouri, Texas, Wisconsin, and Wyoming, allow for jury trials (usually in the adjudication and/or termination phases). Advocates have reported to the Juvenile Law Society that even where authorized, jury cases are rare. www.juvenilelawsociety.org.

percent of judges surveyed wanted lawyers to formulate evidence into more cohesive stories.[3]

The Legal Framework of a Child Welfare Case

The Federal Model

Child welfare is governed by state law, and state child welfare law is derived from federal child welfare law.[4] The federal government, through the Department of Health and Human Services, Administration of Children, Youth, and Families (The Children's Bureau) provides significant financial incentives to states that conform to the federal model. All U.S. jurisdictions have adopted state child welfare law that conforms to this federal model. While differences in law do exist from state to state, particularly within code organization and terminology, the foundational framework is uniform. Additionally, there is a significant body of federal constitutional case law that defines the relationship between parents and children, parents and the state, and children and the state.[5]

Child welfare law has evolved from the first federal enactment in 1974,[6] which emphasized child protection and removal, to family preservation (reasonable efforts) in 1980,[7] which stressed family services, to the safety-plus permanence laws of 1997.[8] The current law as prescribed by Congress and adopted by the states sets forth the following three goals of the child welfare system:

Safety

Safety is the clearest and most measurable of all the goals. The goal of safety is to ensure that the child is free from abuse and neglect.

Permanence

The goal of permanence recognizes that children are harmed by living in the limbo of temporary foster care, particularly when they are moved multiple times.

3. "Are Judges Becoming More Like Jurors," Ken Broda Bahm, PhD, Persuasion Strategies National Surveys 2008, A Service of Holland and Hart, LLP, Denver, CO, www.persuasionstrategies.com.

4. MARVIN VENTRELL & DONALD DUQUETTE, CHILD WELFARE LAW AND PRACTICE: REPRESENTING CHILDREN, PARENTS, AND STATE AGENCIES IN ABUSE, NEGLECT, AND DEPENDENCY CASES 143 (Bradford 2005).

5. *Id.* at 185.

6. CHILD ABUSE PREVENTION AND TREATMENT ACT (CAPTA), 42 U.S.C. § 5101.

7. ADOPTION ASSISTANCE AND CHILD WELFARE ACT (96-272), 42 U.S.C. § 620.

8. ADOPTION AND SAFE FAMILIES ACT (ASFA), 42 U.S.C. § 101.

The law prioritizes permanent placement, beginning with the child's family. Family preservation (through the provision of "reasonable efforts") remains a system goal and is coupled with the constitutional law that parentage is a fundamental liberty interest.

Well-Being

Well-being is a largely subjective goal and allows for argument that a child's best interests can be served through various outcomes.

The system goals of safety, permanence, and well-being give rise to the following broad child welfare case themes:

- The *safety* of the child is our paramount concern.

- Children do not thrive in temporary care so a ***permanent*** home for the child must be established as soon as possible.

- Children thrive and belong with their parents, and all ***reasonable efforts*** must be made to preserve the family.

- Children thrive in ***permanent*** care with loving and competent caretakers, even if those caretakers were once strangers to them.

- The ***well-being*** or best interests of the child require a particular outcome.

These system themes exist within a complex child welfare court process that proceeds through various stages. The stages vary by state but generally include:

1. Preliminary Protective Hearing (a/k/a Removal, Temporary Custody, Detention)
   Issue: Is the child abused, neglected, or dependent?
   Standard of Proof: Probable cause.[9]

2. Adjudication
   Issue: Is the child abused, neglected, or dependent?
   Standard of Proof: Preponderance of the evidence.

3. Disposition
   Issue: What current placement and service plan are in the child's best interests?
   Standard of Proof: Preponderance of the evidence.

---

9. Standards of proof may vary by jurisdiction. Termination of parental rights requires a clear and convincing evidence standard by U.S. Supreme Court ruling. *See, e.g.,* Santosky v. Kramer, 455 U.S. 745 (1982). The Indian Child Welfare Act (ICWA) provides for specific standards.

4. Review / Permanency
   Issue: What is the status of the child and the permanency plan?
   Standard of Proof: Preponderance of the evidence.

5. Termination of Parental Rights (TPR)
   Issue: Should the parent's rights be terminated?
   Standard of Proof: Clear and convincing evidence.

6. Adoption or Guardianship
   Issue: Will this permanent placement serve the child's best interests?
   Standard of Proof: Preponderance of the evidence.

In practice, adjudication and disposition are frequently combined such that disposition follows immediately on the heels of adjudication, assuming the child is adjudicated. Adjudication, disposition, and TPR are the child welfare proceedings that are most like traditional trials in terms of the calling of witnesses and presentation of evidence. Most case analysis in child welfare focuses on these proceedings.

Jury Instructions and Findings and Conclusions

State statutory law and state case law, as modeled after the federal law, define the law of the case. This law must be incorporated by the child welfare courtroom lawyer into jury instructions (instructions) in jury trials and findings of fact and conclusions of law (findings) in bench trials. These instructions and findings should be referred to early and often when preparing for trial.

Case Theory, Theme, and Story Devices

The story of the case is comprised of three parts: case theory, case theme, and case story devices.

Case Theory

The theory of the case is comprised of the legal elements of the case in their bare fact form. It is the essential foundation of the case without any persuasive packaging. Before moving forward, counsel must be absolutely clear about the theory that must be proved or refuted. Before moving to a child welfare case example, a traditional criminal homicide matter will help to illustrate the concept of case theory as follows:

1. The identified defendant John Doe,

2. On July 15, 201_,

3. In the county of Nita, state of Nita,

4. With intent to cause serious bodily harm,

5. Fired a revolver at Jane Doe,

6. Causing her death.

These elements, if proved beyond a reasonable doubt, form the legal theory of the case and warrant a guilty verdict. Similarly, the elements of a dependency court adjudication action, if proved by a preponderance of the evidence, warrant a finding of abuse and neglect.

Case Theme

While theoretically sufficient for a conviction, experience has taught prosecutors that convictions can rarely be gained by theory alone. Rather, it is human nature to ask for more—an explanation of how and why something happened. In other words, judges and jurors need to be persuaded that these bare facts are true. This persuasion or explanation is the theme of the case. In our criminal scenario, the theme might go like this:

> John Doe, a veteran of the Afghan war, returned home to his wife, Jane. Since returning home, Mr. and Ms. Doe have not been getting along, and John Doe has become increasingly agitated with Jane for having friends and a new life, which she acquired while he was gone. After a long day of work on a highway road crew on a sweltering hot summer day, July 15, 201_, followed by several rounds of beers, John Doe entered the couple's home in Nita City, Nita, and heard Jane say to someone on the phone, "I have to go now; I love you too." He angrily confronted Jane and would not accept her explanation that she was talking to her friend Ann Smith and not another man. He went to the kitchen drawer, pulled out his revolver, pointed it at Jane and told her to tell the truth now. Jane screamed "NO, DON'T," and reached for the gun. Enraged in anger and jealousy, John Doe fired three shots at his wife, killing her instantly. Police responded to a neighbor's call that gunshots were heard at the Doe house. Upon entering the home, police found Jane's dead body on the kitchen floor and John Doe sitting silently at the kitchen table with the gun in his hand at his side.

After hearing the case theme, the fact finder is in a position to say, "Yes, that makes sense; now I can see how that could have happened." This is because the "how" and the "why" of the case have been provided in the form of a story. Working backward from this theme, one can extract the bare facts of the legal theory unchanged.

The same applies to defending a case. While it may be legally correct that a defendant need not prove innocence and may simply hold the state to its burden of proof, few defense attorneys would rely on this. The defendant too, must provide an explanation, the "how" and the "why" of what happened.

Using the theme consistently is also important. Conventional wisdom suggests that the lawyer choose one theme and adhere to it throughout the trial. Having only one theme allows the lawyer to filter all evidence and issues efficiently through that theme. If the evidence supports our theme, we present it. If it does not support our theme, it is excluded as irrelevant.

Moreover, single-theme wisdom presumes that fact finders are not persuaded and may be dissuaded from either/or propositions. To argue that a certain scenario is the explanation, but then offer another scenario as a backup, may well harm one's credibility. As an example, a trial lawyer and NITA instructor once closed his case by discrediting the opposition because of its multiple alternate themes. The lawyer told the jury a fable about a farmer who raised cabbages and his neighbor's goat who ate the cabbages. He said that if the other side were defending that case they would argue:

> I have no goat, but
>
> If I had a goat he would not eat cabbages, and
>
> If he ate cabbages he would not eat yours, and
>
> If he did eat yours it was an accident, and
>
> If it wasn't an accident, then the goat must have gone crazy.[10]

Note: Case themes are not invented; they are real. Lawyers do not create case themes; lawyers uncover case themes from the facts of the case. If the facts do not support a theme, the lawyer is ethically bound to discard that theme.

Story Devices

Additionally, the case story can be enhanced and made more persuasive by using story devices (sometimes confused by lawyers as the theme itself). Story devices are storytelling phrases or analogies that give the listener a touchstone or shorthand means of holding on to the case theme. In our criminal matter, a story device might be something like:

> *The war followed John Doe home.*

---

10. NITA instructor Robert Hanley used this fable when he represented MCI against AT&T in that landmark antitrust case. MCI prevailed.

Be cautious with story devices. While such devices can be compelling, they must pass the "eye roll" test. We lawyers must not get too creative for our own good such that the listener is inclined to roll his eyes at our analogy. It is always wise to test one's story device on friends, family, and colleagues.

Be wary as well of seemingly compelling story devices that can be turned around by opposing counsel. You not only lose your persuasive edge—the opposition improves theirs. Consider how you would respond if confronted with the particular device or analogy.

Using these traditional trial advocacy concepts, we can now see their application in child welfare cases in the form of the following case analysis tools.

Case Analysis Tools

The following instruments are presented as tools that can be used to formulate the story of the case.[11] They are as follows:

1. Case Analysis Summary (CAS)

2. Good Fact / Bad Facts Chart (GFBF)

3. Proof Chart (PC)

Case Analysis Summary (CAS)

A CAS is a means by which to record the story of the case. (*See* next page.)

Good Facts / Bad Facts Chart (GFBF)

Facts make the case. Some facts support your position—those are good facts. Some facts detract from your position—those are bad facts. Some facts cut both ways and can be considered neutral facts or both good and bad. Still, all the facts must be reckoned with in the case analysis process. This can be done by completing a GFBF Chart.

When preparing your GFBF chart, reserve judgment on how powerful the fact is or even whether it will come into evidence. It is important to simply record all the

---

11. The following illustrations are presented from the perspective of the agency attorney, who has the duty to prove the case. It is no less important, however, that parent and child counsel complete their own case analysis forms. When refuting agency claims, counsel should indicate in the case theory section, not just that an element is unmet, but also any contrary affirmative fact.

known facts that may become relevant. By reserving value judgments at the outset, you can perform a more objective case analysis.

Sample Agency Attorney Dependency Case Analysis Summary (CAS) Form

Case: *In the Matter of LME, A Minor*
Stage: Adjudication
Issue: Whether LME suffered "physical abuse" while in mother's care
Proof: Preponderance of the evidence

Theory / Legal Elements of State Code Section 1234
1. LME is a minor
2. Was in the care of Ms. Ellen, her bio mother
3. One January 15, 201_
4. In Nita County, Nita
5. Suffered a broken collar bone
6. Caused by falling down the stairs after being pushed by Ms. Ellen

Theme / Story Framework (how could this have happened?)
LME is a ten-year-old girl with ADHD. Ms. Ellen is a single mother who works full time. Ms. Ellen is the adult child of an alcoholic with severe anger management issues. LME pushes her buttons and tries her patience. After a sleepless night and full day of work as a waitress, Ms. Ellen came home and found LME acting out and demanding to go to McDonald's. Ms. Ellen snapped, grabbed LME, shook her, and pushed her down the stairs. LME suffered scrapes and bruises and a broken collarbone.

Storytelling Devices / Analogies
1. *Life in a pressure cooker; something has got to give*
2. *Anger kills*

---

* * *

**Sample Agency Attorney Dependency Case Analysis
Good Facts / Bad Facts Chart (GFBF) Form**

Good Facts	/	*Bad Facts*
1. Broken Collar Bone		1. Injury is consistent with accidental fall
2. LME has ADHD		2. Mom works hard to support LME
3. Mom has anger issues		3. Child is only witness
4. Mom is stressed		4. No previous history of abuse
5. Child is difficult		5. Child is difficult

Ultimately, it is critical that you not ignore or wish away bad facts. While you may choose not to present a bad fact, it is nonetheless part of the case. Denying the existence of bad facts leads to false themes that do not hold up under scrutiny.

Proof Chart (PC)

The PC is the means by which a lawyer organizes and records the presentation of evidence. A PC should, at a minimum, list the facts and elements that must be proved and the manner of proof (which witnesses and exhibits prove the various elements). You may want to customize your PCs to include such details as where in the pretrial record the fact can be found and a reminder to evaluate how the fact promotes the case theme.

Sample Agency Attorney Dependency Case Analysis Proof Chart (PC) Form			
Fact/Element	**Proved By/ Location**	**Proved With (Exhibit)**	**Matches Theme**
1. The Injury	Dr. Welby / Med. Record	Ex. 1 (x-ray)	Yes
2. ADHD	Teacher / Statement	Ex. 2 (Meds OK Slip)	Yes
3. Mom's anger	Caseworker / Police Rpt.	None	Yes
4. Mom's job stress	Mom / SW Interview	None	Yes
5. Push caused fall	LME / Adv. Center	None	Yes

Getting Started

There is some debate on the order and manner of case analysis. Some lawyers believe that the first step must be the completion of a Good Facts / Bad Facts Chart before a case theory and theme is proposed. The rationale for this view is that an objective recitation of the facts must precede any analysis, lest the facts be made to fit a preconceived story. Others believe that the recitation of good and bad facts is not possible without at least a preliminary theory in place that gives context to what *is* a good or a bad fact. However one proceeds, it is imperative to check one's case story against the actual facts. The dangers of not doing so are the creation of a false story and the failure to address existing facts.

The following order of case analysis is suggested:

1. Perform a basic file review.

2. State the issue.

3. Prepare a preliminary Case Analysis Summary (CAS).

4. Complete a Good Facts / Bad Facts Chart (GFBF).

5. Review preliminary case story from the CAS in light of your Good Facts / Bad Facts and make necessary adjustments.

6. Complete the Proof Chart (PC).

7. Review and Finalize the CAS.

This order and manner of case analysis presents essentially a legal version of the scientific method in which a hypothesis is formed and tested. Once case analysis is complete, the following formula should apply:

> *Case Theory + Case Theme = Case Story + the Law of the Case*
> *= Desired Outcome*

Having completed the case analysis process, the child welfare lawyer may turn his attention to preparing the foundation of the case, direct examination. The following overall order of case preparation is suggested.[12]

1. Case Analysis

2. Direct Examination (including Expert Witness Direct and Exhibits)[13]

3. Closing Argument

4. Cross-Examination

5. Objections Preparation

6. Opening Statement

---

12. The suggested case preparation sequence corresponds to the order in which the chapters appear in this book.

13. Some lawyers believe that closing argument preparation should precede direct examination preparation.

CHAPTER TWO

DIRECT EXAMINATION
THE WORDS OF THE STORY

I keep six honest serving-men:

(They taught me all I knew)

*Their names are **What** and **Where** and **When***

*And **How** and **Why** and **Who** . . . . .*[1]

Take-Away

*Tell the witness's part of the story with nonleading
sensory perception questions divided by topic and headlines.*

Direct examination is the essential element of the trial. It is the means by which the case is proved. If a trial is a story, then the direct examination constitutes the words of the story. There are many parts of the trial where a case is lost, but only one part where the case is won: direct examination.

Direct examination is the foundation of the case from which all other parts of the case are derived. In opening statement, we foreshadow what will be said in direct examination. In cross-examination, we attempt to marginalize that which may limit our evidence on direct examination. In closing argument, we apply the law to the evidence we elicited on direct and argue why that demands a finding for our client. All of these are derivatives of direct examination.

Direct examination tells the story of the case through the witnesses' words, sometimes enhanced by visual aids and the physical evidence the witnesses use. In child welfare court, witnesses typically include parents, foster parents, extended family, social workers, teachers, therapists, neighbors, doctors, law enforcement professionals, and children themselves. Each of these witnesses tells a unique and potentially powerful part of the story of the family.

---

1. RUDYARD KIPLING, *The Elephant's Child* (emphasis added). Thank you Mark Caldwell, NITA Program Director, for identifying this reference.

The Rule of Sensory Perception of Facts

The substance of a witness's testimony on direct examination should be factual information that the witness possesses, having acquired such information through the senses. Senses are the physiological methods of human perception, typically consisting of sight, sound, feel, hearing, and taste. When we add to these the witness's actions (i.e., What did you do? *I ran, I hid, I screamed for help*), the substance of direct examination is formed.

Topics for direct examination, therefore, consist primarily of a witness's immediate perceptions and actions. Children may testify as to what was done to them or what they saw done to a sibling. Parents may testify as to their parenting actions and observations of the other parent's conduct. Caseworkers may testify as to what they observed during an investigation and, with certain hearsay limitations, what they heard from others.

This focus on the witness testifying from experience can be thought of as *the rule of sensory perception*, and it can be illustrated by the exception to the rule: lay witness opinion. As a general rule, lay or fact witnesses are not allowed to give opinions and must testify about facts. The exception is a proper lay witness opinion where a fact witness, not qualified as an expert witness, may opine on a matter only if it is rationally based on the witness's *perception*. A social worker may be allowed to testify not only that a child cried during a scheduled visitation (clearly an observed fact), but also that the child was distressed (an opinion of condition based on the observed fact of crying). The latter may be seen as a proper lay witness opinion because, while not technically a factual observation, it is an opinion that is nonetheless "rationally based on the *perception* of the witness."[2]

Conversely, the same caseworker would likely not be allowed to testify that a mother of a child disliked her (dislike being a subjective emotional opinion), but could testify about facts consistent with the condition of dislike, such as name-calling. Effective direct examination, therefore, requires that the examiner seek to elicit facts and not opinions or conclusions.

Understanding this distinction is aided by differentiating direct examination from closing argument. It is unpersuasive and arguably objectionable to attempt to elicit a caseworker's opinion or conclusion that a parent was uncooperative. Lack of cooperation is better proved by eliciting from the witness a series of facts, such as: *the father used abusive language*; *he missed 90 percent of his appointments*; *he failed to return any phone calls*; *he refused to attend parenting classes*. These are the facts that lead to the conclusion that the parent was uncooperative. Then, during closing

---

2. FED. R. EVID. 701.

argument, the lawyer may recite those facts and draw the conclusion that the parent is uncooperative. Failure to distinguish facts from conclusions, coupled with a hurried desire to elicit a quick conclusion without building the facts for the record, may be the most common and problematic error on direct examination.

> *Failure to distinguish facts from conclusions*
> *—coupled with a hurried desire to elicit a quick*
> *conclusion without building the facts for the record—*
> *may be the most common and problematic error of the*
> *lawyer on direct examination.*

The key to successful direct examination of a fact witness, therefore, is focus on the witness's direct personal perceptions and actions and not their opinions, conclusions, or feelings.

Case Analysis

Prepare for direct examination by determining which witnesses to call, in which order to call them, and what to ask them. Having engaged in the case analysis process from the outset, you have combined the legal theory (the elements of the case) with a persuasive explanation (the theme) to form the story of the family. Direct examination calls on us to determine the most persuasive way to organize the telling of the story through the witnesses. At this point, refer to your Proof Chart (*see* Case Analysis, chapter one) and organize the calling of the witnesses in the most persuasive order, based on which elements of the story each witness can best tell.

It is imperative to not overvalue a witness's scope of information. A witness knows what he or she knows and no more. You can disrupt the flow of the case and cause serious damage to it by overstating what the witness can say. Witness credibility must be paramount at all times.

Focus on the Witness

Because direct examination is an opportunity for a witness to tell part of the story of the case in the witness's own words, describing the witness's direct experience and perceptions, it is the witness—not the lawyer—who must be the focus of direct examination. This is the opposite of cross-examination. It is lawyer's job on direct to highlight the witness in such a way that the witness can tell his or her part of the story in the most persuasive possible fashion.

> **It can be useful at this point to check our work against five basic questions:**
>
> 1. Is the testimony I plan to elicit entirely consistent with **theory and theme**?
>
> 2. Is this the **best witness** from whom to elicit this information?
>
> 3. Is the information **relevant** to proving the case theory and theme?
>
> 4. Does the witness possess the requisite legal **foundation** to testify about this information?
>
> 5. Is the statement **hearsay**, and if so, is there an exception to allow the testimony?
>
> *Once these five criteria are satisfied, you should prepare the direct examination.*

Imagine hearing a compelling story about a real-life event. As the storyteller proceeds, you become engaged and want to know what is going to happen. The storyteller pauses. At that point, you ask, "And then what happened?" In a sense, that is what the lawyer does in direct exam—he prompts the witness through the storytelling process.

Of course the lawyer does a great deal more than just ask *what happened next.* Witnesses are not allowed to narrate their testimony, but rather must respond to specific questions. So it is the lawyer's job to headline story topics and then prompt the witness to give succinct and responsive segments of the story through short, open-ended, nonleading questions.

It is sometimes suggested that direct examination should be like a conversation. This is true in the sense that on direct the witness should use conversational language to describe her observations and actions. It is at best a very one-sided conversation, where the witness provides all of the information. Remember—the focus is on the witness, not the lawyer.

Witness Preparation

The witness, therefore, has a difficult job to do. She is asked, typically with little if any communication training or familiarity with the court process, to thoroughly and clearly describe important information to the fact finder. It is also likely that the witness has an interest in the outcome and has significant anxiety about testifying. It is your job, therefore, to prepare the witness by making sure the witness knows the substantive information that will be requested and helping the witness become comfortable with the role of providing persuasive facts.

Witness preparation is allowed and expected in the U.S. by court convention. While it is unethical to "coach" a witness by telling a witness what to say—or worse, encouraging false testimony[3]—you should talk to your direct examination witness about what you will be asking the witness and how you will ask it. Assure the witness that it is appropriate to prepare. Be sure to explain to witnesses that they are required to tell the truth and that they may ask for clarification, restatement, or simply answer, "I don't know" or "I don't understand the question" where appropriate.

Because very little discovery is conducted in child welfare court, it is even more important to prepare witnesses for court testimony in these types of cases. This, combined with the reality that child welfare court witnesses are difficult to access and lawyers typically have inadequate time to prepare witnesses, is a serious systemic flaw. While system policy change is not the subject of this publication, there can be no doubt that effective direct examination is tied to the level of witness preparation. This can be particularly acute on occasions where a child witness is called to testify.

The Rule and Reason Against Leading Questions

Leading questions are prohibited on direct examination, with minor exceptions.[4] Apart from the statutory prohibition against leading the witness on direct examination, leading questions are an ineffective technique because they detract from the witness's ability to tell a story.

Leading questions ask merely for the witness to confirm or deny that which the questioner has stated. The leading question, "The house was filthy, correct?," instructs the investigator witness to confirm the questioner's belief and no more. Yet it is not the questioning lawyer's belief about which we should be concerned. We should be concerned about what the witness knows and volunteered without being

---

3. MODEL RULES OF PROF'L CONDUCT, R. 3.4(b).

4. FED. R. EVID. 611(c): "Leading questions should not be used on direct examination of a witness except as may be necessary to develop the witness' testimony." Such exceptions typically include, by convention and common law, foundation for further testimony, foundation for introduction of exhibits, preliminary matters, questions for the very young and very old, and the efficient development of testimony (headlining). *See* People v. Petschow, 119 P.3d 495 (2005).

told to what to recall. Testifying from one's independent recollection is a fundamental tenant of our evidentiary system. It is also the most persuasive form of storytelling and communication with the fact finder.

Question form can be separated into three types:

1. Leading

   Q: The house was *filthy*, correct?

   A: Yes.

The question contains the answer and instructs the witness to agree to the answer.

2. Suggesting

   Q: Was the house *filthy*?

   A: Yes.

The question contains the answer and arguably suggests it to the witness. Some courts may consider this a leading question.

3. Open

   Q: What was the condition of the house?

   A: It was *filthy*. I was actually uncomfortable going in there. It smelled horrible. There were dirty clothes strewn about the floor. There were dozens of dirty dishes with left-over food on them. The garbage was overflowing onto the floor. Flies were everywhere. It was really awful.

This question neither suggests nor contains the answer. It calls on the witness to recall and articulate the answer. It also allows and even encourages the witness to engage in responsive, descriptive storytelling. It is, therefore, this "open" type question that satisfies not just the law, but also the purpose of direct. Open questions should comprise the vast majority of questions asked on direct examination.

Questioning Techniques[5]

Use Six Honest Words

Rudyard Kipling referred to "six honest men" in connection with the six words **what, where, when, how, why, who.** They are honest words because when one

---

5. The techniques of Six Honest Words, Headlines, and Loopbacks are attributable to and part of NITA training.

seeks information with them, they prohibit the questioner from imposing or suggesting the answer. Questions formed with these words are necessarily fair questions. Questions formed with these words cannot be leading questions. As such, they should be the first words of the majority of questions on direct examination.

Avoid the natural tendency to use the words: "is," "was," "did," and "were" to begin a direct examination question. The questions: "Is the house filthy?" "Was the house filthy?" "Did you see the filthy house?" or "Were you at the filthy house?" all contain the sought-after information, are suggestive, call for a confirmation and not a persuasive answer, and may be seen as leading.

It can be challenging to construct a direct examination with only the six honest words. Experience and practice will make the task easier. The occasional suggestive transitional question will help the process (Did you visit the house?), as will the liberal use of headlines and the occasional use of the phrases: "please describe" or "please explain," as in: "Please describe the condition of the house."

Use Headlines

Headlines, sometimes called headnotes, are extremely useful to the organization and flow of the direct examination. It is difficult to construct a direct examination using only open-ended, nonleading questions without this tool. Headlines direct the witness and allow the fact finder to better follow the examination. They serve as transitions between topic areas. Headlines are sometimes described as the chapter titles to the book that is the story of the case.

Headlines are statements by the lawyer directing the witness to a particular topic—they typically begin with phrases such as: *let's talk about . . .*; *I'd like to ask you some questions about . . .*; and, *I'd like to refer you to . . . .* In this way, the lawyer sets up a series of questions about a particular topic without asking a leading question, alerting the witness and fact finder of the change in topic. It also allows the fact finder to refocus attention, which might have wandered. It is important to use headlines properly—don't try to place facts in the record by using the headline to sneak in argumentative facts or conclusions or facts not in evidence.

While headlines are used regularly in courts throughout the U.S. by convention, you may occasionally be faced with an objection that you are testifying or not asking a question. The headline is not testimony so long as it does not include facts not in evidence. Further, headlines should be allowed as proper examination organization that simply alerts the witness (and the fact finder) to the area of questioning that would follow.

The illustration that resonates with many judges is the time-honored headline by the prosecutor: "Officer, I would like to direct your attention to the afternoon of

April 1, 201_." While not a question, it is universally accepted as a proper organizational and directive questioning technique. Additional legal authority exists for headlines in that "the court shall exercise reasonable control over the mode . . . of interrogating witnesses and presenting evidence so as to (1) make the interrogation and presentation effective . . . ."[6] Further, some leading of witnesses on direct may be allowed "as may be necessary to develop . . . testimony."[7]

Use Loopbacks

Loopback questions are effective to focus the witness and fact finder and to emphasize an important fact already in evidence. They are used as a predicate or condition to a question. They are permissible because they are part of a proper nonleading question, are not argumentative, and do not assume facts not in evidence. Assume, for example, that a caseworker testified that a father was uncooperative with the investigation. A follow-up, loopback question would be: "You said earlier that the father was uncooperative; how was he uncooperative?" One might even combine a loopback question with a headline transition: "You stated on direct that the father was uncooperative; I'd like to ask you some questions about that."

Organization

The Three Parts of Direct Examination

It is useful to organize and divide direct examination of fact witnesses into three basic parts:

    1. Introduce and accredit the witness;

    2. Ask the witness to set the scene; and

    3. Ask the witness to describe the action.

1. Introduce and Accredit the Witness

To persuade the fact finder that the witness should be believed, the fact finder must have an appreciation for the witness: who the witness is, why the witness is here, why the witness knows the information, and why the witness should be trusted and believed. This is the role of introduction and accreditation, and lawyers frequently minimize it as a mere formality. You should take adequate time, without belaboring the obvious or delving into irrelevant or minor details, to establish the credibility of the witness through introduction and accreditation.

---

6. FED. R. EVID. 611(a).

7. FED. R. EVID. 611(c).

The following codes are used to illustrate technique:

Bold Word = One of the seven honest words

Bold Sentence = *Headline*

Italics= Loopback

Good morning.

Q: Please tell us your name?

A: My Name is Theresa Gordon.

Q: **Where** do you live Ms. Gordon?

A: Right here in Nita City.

Q: **How** long have you lived in Nita City?

A: All my life, except for when I left for college.

Q: **How** old are Ms. Gordon?

A: I'm thirty-nine years old.

Q: **Where** do you work?

A: Nita Elementary School.

Q: **What** do you do at Nita Elementary School?

A: I'm the third grade teacher.

Q: **How** long have you worked at Nita Elementary?

A: Seventeen years.

Q: **How** long have you taught third grade?

A: I've taught third grade for most of that time, the last ten years anyway.

Q: Ms. Gordon, do you know a child named Victoria Jones?

A: Yes I do.

Q: **How** do you know Victoria?

A: I'm her teacher.

Q: **Why** are you here today Ms. Gordon?

A: I was asked to come here and testify regarding my observations of Victoria in my class.

Before you do that, I'd like to ask you a few questions about your teaching qualifications.

Q: *Ms. Gordon, you mentioned earlier that you left Nita City to go to college*; **where** did you go to college?

A: Nita State.

Q: **What**, if any, degree did you obtain?

A: I received a BA in Elementary Education with a minor in Spanish.

Q: **How** did you do in college?

A: Very well I think. I love education, learning and teaching, and I graduated with high honors.

Q: Ms. Gordon, as part of your preparation for teaching, **what**, if any, courses did you take regarding young children's behavior.

A: I took several, including the core requirement called child and adolescent behavior and psychology.

Q: **What** is child and adolescent behavior and psychology?

A: It is the study of normal and abnormal behavioral patterns and what causes those patterns.

Q: *You said this was a core requirement*; **why** is it considered important?

A: Two reasons. First, it impacts a child's ability to learn, and second, it helps teachers identify children in potential crisis.

Q: **What**, if any, other courses or training have you had in identifying children in potential crisis?

A: Several. Most notably I took the Nita School District mandatory training on recognizing signs of child maltreatment.

Q: Ms. Gordon, **why** are you a teacher?

A: Simple—I love kids. I love helping them reach their potential.

* * *

The forgoing sample examination illustrates how a teacher can be presented to a fact finder as relevant, interesting, and credible. Such examinations should be shortened or expanded based on the facts and story of the case. Do not be deterred by the occasional impatience of the court and opposing counsel on such matters. While it is advisable to be respectful of the court's time and to never waste time, it is the duty of the lawyer to persuade within the rules and court conventions. A lawyer may, on such occasions, advise the court that the lawyer respects the courts time, but that it is important to hear a reasonable amount of the witness's background because it will relate to testimony about maltreatment and thereby assist the court.

2. Ask the Witness to Set the Scene

Scene setting is that portion of direct examination that leads up to the action, places the witness in the action, and provides further and more specific foundation for the ultimate action testimony. It may overlap a bit with the accreditation information of part 1.

Ms. Gordon, I'd like to ask you some questions now about the morning of Tuesday, November 20, 201_.

Q: Do you remember that morning?

A: Yes, I do.

Q: **Where** were you at approximately 8:00 a.m.?

A: I was at the school.

Q: **What** time did you get to school?

A: My usual time, about 7:00 a.m.

Q: **What** did you do?

A: A little busy work, housekeeping matters first.

Q: **What** did you do next?

A: I got out my roll call book and reviewed my lesson plan for the day.

Q: **When** did the children arrive for school?

A: The bell rings at 8:10, and they come into the classroom by 8:15.

Q: **What** did you do once the children arrived?

A: I took roll.

Q: **What** did you find out from your roll call?

A: That all sixteen of my students were in the class except one.

Q: **Who** was absent?

A: Victoria Jones.

Q: **What** did you do next?

A: Well, because the office had not informed me that I had any absences, I told the children to be still, that I would be right back, and I went to the office to turn in my roll sheet and advise them that Victoria was absent.

Q: **What** happened when you went to the office?

A: I never made it to the office.

Q: **Why** not?

A: Because when I opened my door, I saw Victoria standing there in the hall all by herself.

Ms. Gordon, before we talk about what happened after you discovered Victoria in the hall, I want to talk about what kind of student Victoria is in your class.

Q: How long have you known Victoria?

A: I have known her since she started school here three years ago as a kindergartner.

Q: How long have you been her teacher?

A: Since the beginning of this school year, so about three months.

Q: What kind of student is she?

A: She's a good student.

Q: Why do you say that?

A: Because she is socially well adjusted and does well academically.

You mentioned two things just now, let's take those one at a time, starting with social adjustment.

Q: **What** do you mean when you say she is socially well adjusted?

A: She interacts with the other students and the teachers very well, has friends, and easily participates in activities.

Q: *You also described her as a good student,* **why**?

A: She regularly and eagerly participates in class, does her work, and gets A's and B's in her subjects.

Q: **What** if any behavioral problems have you had with Victoria?

A: None.

Let's talk now about Victoria's family.

Q: **How** do you know the family, if you do?

A: I do; I met Victoria's parents at the fall parent-teacher conferences.

Q: **Why** do you hold parent-teacher conferences?

A: So that the school, teacher, and parents can all be on the same page participating in the education of the student. Also we find out if there are special family issues.

Q: **What** were your impressions of the parents' ability to be part of this educational team process?

A: Good. They were very cooperative and engaged.

Q: You mentioned earlier that conferences also are held to discover any special family issues. **What**, if any such issues did you discover with Victoria's family?

A: Well, they were concerned about the house being crowded and different because the mother's brother had lost his home to foreclosure and he and his family were coming to live with them. Also, there was some concern about the brother having been in some kind of trouble.

Q: **What** is the brother's name?

A: Sean Watson.

At this point in the examination, the scene is set for something to happen, the fact finder is poised to hear it, and the witness is placed in a position to describe it.

3. Ask the Witness to Describe the Action

The description of the action varies depending on the type of "action" involved. An eyewitness to violence will describe the violent action observed, such as witnessing a parent strike a child in the car of a parking lot. A caseworker may describe the action observed at a supervised visit. Sometimes, action may be less event based, such as a neighbor describing his observations that the family seemed to keep to themselves and were rarely seen coming and going. The action part of direct examination is the reason for calling the witness. The witness must describe the action with such clarity and precision that the lawyer is certain that the legal elements and the story components for which this witness is responsible have become evidence.

Ms. Gordon, I want to return now and talk to you now about what you saw and what you did once you saw Victoria in the hall on the morning of November 20.

Q: **What** was the very first thing you noticed when you saw Victoria standing in the hall all by herself?

A: Well, it was odd to me that she was out there, and I noticed that she was just standing in the middle of the hall, stiff like a board, just staring at the classroom door.

Q: **What** did you do when you saw her like that?

A: I went to her, spoke to her, and put my arm around her to bring her into the class?

Q: **What** did Victoria do?

A: At first she jerked a little, like she was startled when I touched her.

Q: **What** happened when you took her into the classroom?

A: She was moving a little slowly so it took a minute but I took her to her seat and she sat down.

Now I would like to direct your attention to later the same morning, in your classroom, at about 10:00 a.m.

Q: **What** happened at 10:00 a.m.?

A: Well, the students were to be working quietly by themselves on a project when I heard the students begin to make noise and shuffle about in their desks.

Q: **What** did you do?

A: I asked the students to quiet down and focus on their work.

Q: **How** did the students respond?

A: Not well.

Q: **Why?**

A: Well, I didn't know at first, but then I saw several students pointing at Victoria.

Q: **What** did you do?

A: I looked at Victoria.

Q: **What** did you see?

A: She was crying and shaking.

Q: **What** did you do when you saw her *crying and shaking*?

A: I went to her desk to comfort her and find out what was wrong.

Q: **What** did you find out?

A: Well, that Victoria was clearly very distressed and that she had had an accident—she had urinated all over herself and the desk seat.

Q: **How** did you respond to this?

A: Well, I was surprised and concerned. I took steps to comfort Victoria, settle down the class, get a temporary teacher in the class, clean up the desk, and take Victoria to the school nurse.

Let's talk about taking Victoria to the school nurse.

Q: Please describe how you did that.

A: First, I took Victoria to the girls' bathroom, and we got her cleaned up. Then I explained that we were just going to the nurse's office and we would get her some dry things and it that was OK.

Q: **What** did you do next?

A: We knocked on Nurse Smith's door, and she let us in.

Q: **What** did you and Nurse Smith do?

A: We comforted Victoria and asked her if anything was wrong.

Q: **How** did Victoria react?

A: She started crying and shaking and putting her hands between her legs in her crotch, but she would not talk.

Q: **What** did you do next?

A: I called Nita CPS—Child Protective Services.

Q: **Why** did you call Nita CPS?

A: Because I was required to.

Q: **Why** were you *required to* do so?

A: Because school teachers and school nurses are mandatory child abuse reporters.

Q: **What** does that mean, that you are a *mandatory child abuse reporter*?

A: It means that I am legally required to report possible child abuse when I observe known indicators of it.

Q: **Where** are these *known indicators* found?

A: In the Nita School District training materials and procedures guide.

Q: **What** indicators found in your guidelines did you observe with Victoria?

A: I observed four.

Q: **What** was the fist?

A: Standing in the hall by herself, after class had begun, appearing shocked.

Q: **What** was the second?

A: Urinating on herself.

Q: **What** was the third?

A: Inability to answer questions about what happened or why she was distressed.

Q: And **what** was the fourth?

A: Holding her crotch.

Q: Ms. Gordon, **what** happened after you called CPS?

A: A CPS investigator arrived at the school to meet with Victoria.

No further questions at this time, your Honor.

Thank you, Ms. Gordon.

By the close of the direct examination, the witness has described the event or events she perceived, in her own words, as prompted and organized by her lawyer. Any testimony that is not unquestionably a fact is rationally based on the witness's perception. The witness has told her part of the story of the family.

Sequencing within the Topic

Events are best understood when presented in a logical, orderly sequence. It is difficult to understand stories told out of order. Make your direct examination points in a sequence where questions build one upon another, in order, leading to an ending. In the example of Ms. Gordon's testimony above, the sequence begins with Ms. Jones training, moves to her job as a teacher; she then meets Victoria, learns about her family, observes Victoria as a good student, notices something is wrong, investigates, and reports child abuse. These events build each from the prior and follow each other.

At the same time, however, we want to tell compelling and persuasive stories, and this calls for some variability of sequence. It is frequently advisable to move from strictly sequential, chronological organization to a topical organization. In our example, while setting the scene in part two, Ms. Gordon reveals that she found Victoria alone in the hall. Next, however, the lawyer changes topics to discuss Victoria's typical conduct as a student so that we can better appreciate what happens when we return to Victoria in the hall. The key is to remain sequential within the topics that may vary in time and place.

Engage: Stop, Look, and Listen

Anxiety can cause the lawyer to focus on a list of questions rather than the witness. When the lawyer is connected to the witness, a meaningful exchange is likely and the fact finder is more likely to engage with the witness as well. As a general rule, the fact finder will look where the lawyer looks, and that should be at the witness on direct examination.

This requires us to engage with the witness and not disengage until there are no further questions. Yet there is a tendency, wedded as we are to our game plan, pen in hand, and notes on the lectern, to disengage from the witness as if we were merely taking inventory of our data. We may look up briefly, ask a question, then, while the witness is answering, we look down, check off our list, and prepare the next question. You are well advised, however, to leave the pen at counsel table, set down the notes nearby in case they are needed, and *engage the witness*. When we listen, the witness's answers will not only cue the next question, they will enable us to follow up naturally and make appropriate and logical deviations from our script.

Visual Aids

If a picture is worth anything close to a thousand words, you are well advised to use one. Visual aids can make a direct examination more effective by clarifying an event. In other words, our book can have pictures.

Visual aids, demonstrative exhibits, and witness demonstrations bring verbal testimony to life. Where possible, a lawyer should use these tools to enhance testimony. A physician who testifies that a child had a twisting fracture consistent with inflicted harm can enhance the testimony by standing and showing the clearly apparent fracture line on an x-ray illuminated by a portable x-ray machine, Elmo, or computer projection, while she explains—and shows how—the white fracture line was caused by a twisting motion. This kind of demonstration by a witness is an effective visual aid itself, and you should encourage witnesses, with the courts permission, to get up and demonstrate an action they observed or in which they participated. Photographs and diagrams are also excellent aids and can be blown up and projected for impact.

Defensive Direct

Lawyers do not make the facts of the case. Nor is it ethical (or our job) to distort them. Acceptance of this reality is a key to good trial work because it acknowledges that something is inconsistent and requires reconciliation. It is likely that every case has some bad facts with which we must acknowledge and deal. Where it is probable that the opposing party will bring up these facts, either in cross-examination or through another witness, it is usually a good idea to deal with them ourselves. When such factual shortcomings are acknowledged honestly and in a nondefensive manner, they may be seen as less significant to the fact finder. This is called defensive direct examination. We should ask, with regard to each witness, whether there are weaknesses that should be acknowledged, explained, or minimized. A good rule of thumb is to ask ourselves whether we would bring out the particular fact if we were on the other side.

Primacy and Recency: Start Strong, End Strong

The principles of primacy and recency have important applications in direct examination. The principles apply to both witness sequence and question/topic sequence. Because we know that fact finders retain best and focus on that which they hear first and last, we should organize witness order and examination topic order so that we start strong and end strong, placing weaker matters in the middle.

Call the strongest (and hopefully most important) witnesses first and last, placing less significant or weaker witnesses in the middle. Organize your examination topics so that the strongest (and hopefully most important) topics are discussed first and last. Be particularly careful to avoid potentially objectionable matters at the beginning and end of an examination. Imagine the damage caused by a sustained objection to the last direct examination question or answer—and the lawyer sheepishly saying, "No further questions," and shuffling back to counsel table.

In the example of Ms. Gordon, the examination builds to the point where Ms. Gordon reveals what she observed of Victoria and how she responded by calling CPS. These are the most powerful points of the examination and the purpose for calling the witness. They are Ms. Gordon's portion of the story of the family.

Check Your Work

Apply the five-part test to again check your work:

1. Is the testimony I plan to elicit entirely consistent with **theory and theme?**

    Yes. It supports the theory that Victoria was sexually abused, possibly by her uncle.

2. Is this the **best witness** from whom to elicit this information?

    Yes. As Victoria's teacher, Ms. Gordon is likable, credible, knowledgeable, and was the witness for the events she describes.

3. Is the information **relevant** to proving the case theory and theme?

    Yes. It tends to prove a fact at issue: Victoria was sexually abused, possibly by her uncle.

4. Does the witness possess the requisite legal **foundation** to testify to this information?

> *Yes. Ms. Gordon describes what she directly perceived and how she acted in*
> *response to what she perceived.*[8]

5.   Is the statement *hearsay*, and if so, is there an exception that would allow
     the testimony?

> *She gives no answer based on an out-of-court statement.*

Redirect Examination

Relax, because on the eighth day God created redirect examination (goes the trial
lawyer adage). Redirect examination gives the lawyer the opportunity to repair
damage caused on cross-examination through rehabilitation, explanation, and new
information. Rehabilitation is the process of reviving an impeached witness's credibility by justifying the inconsistency on which the witness was impeached. Explanation is the process of detailing an alternate understanding or impression of the facts
left by the cross-examiner. On occasion, a lawyer may also be able to provide new
information not previously disclosed on direct, so long as the new information does
not exceed the scope of the cross-examination.

Redirect examination follows cross–examination and is generally allowed by
court convention. It is typically limited to the scope of cross. Redirect examination
is subject to the same rules as direct examination, including the prohibition against
asking leading questions. It is not uncommon, however, to hear lawyers lead the
witness on redirect, perhaps unintentionally, having become accustomed to hearing
leading questions on cross-examination. Still, it is not permitted.

Redirect should be waived where no substantial harm was done on cross, or
where, despite having been harmed, there is nothing that can be done to fix the
problem. Counsel should ask for the opportunity to redirect if the court does not
recognize counsel to do so. Remember to prepare your witness for the possibility of
redirect to avoid confusing your witness.

---

8. Note that Ms. Gordon was not asked to opine as to whether Victoria was abused. She
was not qualified as an expert witness in child abuse and such information would likely be
seen as asking for an expert opinion beyond the scope of permissible lay witness opinion.
Neither is Ms. Gordon asked for a lay witness opinion. Instead, she is asked what happened
and how she acted. Nonetheless, be cautious here and know your jurisdiction. It is possible
that some courts could construe Ms. Gordon's justifications for calling CPS as improper lay
witness opinion, in which event it would be unwise to attempt to end on this point.

CHAPTER THREE

CLOSING ARGUMENT
STORY OF THE CASE + LAW = VERDICT

May I wrap this up for you?

Take-Away
Argue that the facts + law = verdict for your client.
Be brief and clear and show appropriate passion for your position.

Closing argument, also called summation, is the opportunity to summarize the information that the trial produced and argue why it warrants a finding in our client's favor. Having been restrained in the opening statement from arguing conclusions, and then eliciting testimony without an opportunity to comment on it, closing argument finally frees the lawyer to explain what it all means.

Closing argument is a valuable and last opportunity to persuade the fact finder of the validity of one's position. It is the last thing the fact finder will hear (principle of recency) before reaching a conclusion. The opportunity must not be wasted.

Jurors look forward to closing argument. They want to better understand what has occurred during the trial and have ambiguities explained. They want to do the right thing, and they will welcome the help. At the same time, jurors also want to get the trial over, reach a decision, and go home.

In bench trials, judges do not always look forward to closing argument. Many judges abhor the lengthy and overly dramatized closings that some lawyers give. Conversely, judges welcome closings by lawyers who use the opportunity to efficiently and rationally summarize the case, draw appropriate conclusions, and help the judge do his or her job.

The essence of closing argument, therefore, is the lawyer figuratively coming to the judge or jury and saying, "Let me briefly wrap this up for you."

Preparation

We must know our destination in order to reach it. Having conceived of a story of the case and then determined how the evidence can be presented through direct examination, we are in a position to summarize where we plan to be at the conclusion of the trial. Therefore, preparing closing argument early in the case preparation process is an excellent way to be certain we are heading in the right direction and taking the most efficient route to get there.

The process of preparing closing argument forces us to account for all of the evidence that must be presented or refuted. It also allows us to "hear ourselves" tell the story we plan to tell. By doing so, we can check our work by asking: "if I accomplish what I say here, will I prevail?" If the answer is *yes*, we are on our way. If the answer is *no*, we can go back and fill in the blanks.

Yet having prepared a complete and precise road map, we will invariably hit some construction and have to detour. Our closing argument will need to be modified based on the development and discovery of facts before and during trial. Additionally, evidence we anticipated coming in may not, and the converse may also be true. We must, therefore, prepare in advance, but also remain flexible so that the closing argument reflects the final product.

Do not read the closing, do not rely heavily on notes, and do not memorize the closing. Drafting a closing and then reducing the draft to bullet points that may be referenced as necessary is a good technique.

Closing Argument Principles

Brevity

It is difficult to justify or imagine the court allowing a closing argument in a dependency case that exceeds thirty minutes. While more time might be appropriate for jury cases, even a five- to ten-minute closing should be sufficient in bench trials. This is particularly important in jurisdictions where closing arguments are not customarily given. In such court cultures, it is important for counsel to request something like five minutes for summation or closing argument. Judges may even be persuaded by a request to briefly summarize proposed findings and conclusions.

In any event, do not be deterred from asking for an opportunity to give an efficient closing argument merely because the court is busy. Abuse, neglect, and dependency cases dictate the outcome of a child's life, and it is not too much to ask that we take a few minutes to make sure we get it right.

Argument

It is axiomatic to say that the most important part of closing argument is the argument. Yet lawyers sometimes fail to fully argue at this point. A statement is not argument if a witness has said it. That is a rule of thumb for preventing us from arguing in opening statement. In opening statement, we recite what will be said and draw no inferences or conclusions from that. Then, in closing argument, we repeat what has been said and argue what it means. It is the lawyer's job in closing to draw the inferences, make the conclusions, and explain/argue that when the law is applied thereto, a certain outcome must follow. Closing is also the time to argue credibility—why our witness should be believed.

Bookend

Bookending is the practice of conforming both the opening statement and closing argument to the case theme. It provides the fact finder with a complete context in which to place all the evidence. It also reflects consistency, competence, and credibility. You should iterate the case theme early then throughout the closing argument.

Using a storytelling device is a persuasive component of bookending. If the case theme is that a mother was so stressed and so lacked resources that she lost control and abused her child, then the story device introduced in opening might be: "Life was like a pressure cooker, and something had to give." Then, in closing argument, you can put the bookend in place by reintroducing the theme through the story device of the pressure cooker: "Life for this mother was indeed a pressure cooker, and something did give when, on June 15, 201_, all the frustrations of life gave way, and Ms. Jones grabbed her daughter and threw her down the stairs in an uncontrolled fit of anger."

You can then continue describing the evidence and arguing its meaning through this theme context. Using the story device one last time at the completion of the closing is also effective.

Promises Kept and Not Kept

It is useful to remind the fact finder that you made certain promises at the outset of trial regarding the proof that would be presented and that you kept those promises. Use examples. Likewise, it is useful to remind the fact finder that opposing counsel also made promises and failed to keep them.

Exhibits and Audio-Visual

If we went to the trouble to introduce exhibits during the trial, they are important enough to use in closing. Time will not permit all of the exhibits to be used, but the lawyer should choose exhibits that underline the argument. It is very effective to pick up and read from an exhibit as clear and tangible proof of a fact, and then send that exhibit to the jury room or hand it to the judge.

Audio-visual aids (AV) should also be used in closing. Giving the fact finder a final look at a projected photograph of a filthy home can be a powerful image to take away. Additionally, you may wish to use AV for visuals that are not in evidence, such as projecting the adjudication statutory elements and highlight that which has been proved or not proved.

Jury Instructions and Findings

Many traditional trial lawyers believe that it is essential in closing argument to project the verdict form, walk the jury through its questions, and answer them as you wish the jury to do. This applies to child welfare proceedings as well. You should, at a minimum, project the verdict form and indicate, for example, in an adjudication trial, where the jury foreman should check that a parent's conduct constitutes child abuse. Other jury instructions may also be used.

The same principle applies to bench trials. While a judge does not need guidance on how to complete the findings of fact, conclusions of law, and order, using or projecting the portion of one's proposed findings as a means of clearly and succinctly showing the judge that you have proved or disproved elements is highly effective in closing argument. It is, in fact, exactly what the judge wants to hear in closing. Help the judge do his or her job!

Emotion

Be real. False, contrived emotion is ineffective with both judges and juries. Sentimentality is not persuasive. Yet real emotion is appropriate and persuasive. Emotion and passion that matches the circumstances is quite persuasive. Further, a lack of emotion and passion where circumstances would normally evoke such emotion can be misperceived, hurting your credibility.

Having engaged the fact finder at the outset of the trial, and then having built credibility throughout the trial, the lawyer is in an ideal position to connect with the listener in closing.

Don'ts

For the most part, closing argument is unencumbered and freeing for the lawyer. There are only a few rules that must be followed, but these few rules—the *don'ts* of closing argument—should be strictly obeyed. Do not risk objection[1] from opposing counsel or remonstration from the judge during closing argument.

---

1. Objections during closing argument are also covered in the objections chapter.

1. Don't state or argue facts not in evidence.

2. Don't misstate facts.

3. Don't misstate the law.

4. Don't express a personal opinion.

5. Don't argue the Golden Rule.

6. Don't appeal to the jurors' prejudice.

7. Don't exceed the scope of the opposition's closing on rebuttal.

Closing Argument Organization

There is no commonly accepted recipe for closing argument. It is, by definition, a creative process dictated by the specific facts and law of a trial. The following five-part organization may still be useful.

The Grabber and Return to Theme (1)

Do not begin the all-important closing with a disingenuous thank you or dry explanation of the purpose of closing argument. Instead, grab the fact finder, iterate the theme, and hold on tight.

> *A mother's love. That's right, this case **is** about a mother's love. A love so profound that it could penetrate the vice grip that crack-cocaine held on her. A love so profound that when every instinct in her mind, every cell in her body cried out for more drugs, she resisted. Somehow, on what must be like a molecular level, this mother fought the withdrawal, the shame, the ridicule, and now the resistance of the government, so that she could care for her child. Yes, opposing counsel is right, this case is about a mother's love, a love without which she wouldn't be here fighting for her child's life.*

The Facts (2)

Remind the fact finder of the promise you made and show how it was kept by clearly reciting the facts.

> *We promised you at the outset of this trial that we would show you that what happened to this child was an accident—a terrible, unfortunate accident. And that is what we have done. Let's review what we now know . . . .*

The Factual Argument (3)

Closing should include argument about both the facts and the law. The first order of business is to argue why the facts as you presented are to be accepted as the correct version. Here it is important to reference why common sense and simple logic suggest that your version of the facts is believable. Refer to the lack of factual evidence to the contrary. Also, make arguments as to why your witnesses on the matter are more credible than the other side's witnesses.

Petitioner should anticipate the obvious factual arguments that respondent counsel will make. Respondent counsel should rebut factual arguments made by the petitioner.

> *Burns of this nature and degree on a small child are not accidental. We know this from the testimony of the emergency room pediatric burn doctor who explained that this child had to have been placed in the scalding tub by another person. We know this because the caseworker, an expert in child development, explained to us that this child was incapable of pulling himself up and falling into the tub. We also know this because the father's explanation is not consistent with the injury. The lack of splash marks tells us that the child did not fall in the tub and struggle until he was found.*

The Legal Argument (4)

The purpose of arguing the law is to connect the facts to the outcome. You should use the jury instructions to argue the law and its application to the facts to the jury. In a bench trial, argue both statutory and case law to the court. Consider a brief argument on standard of proof. Petitioners may want to emphasize standard of proof where it is low, and respondents where the standard is high.

> *Your Honor, the law is unequivocal in the state of Nita that once basic safety is assured, preservation of the family is the goal. Section 1-1-101 of our child welfare code states that all reasonable efforts must be made to provide appropriate reunification services to a family. These parents are imperfect but want desperately to parent their children. Their testimony and the admissions by the caseworker showed that. And the law says they have a right to parent their children and that their children have a right to be parented by them. The court's dispositional order must include a legitimate opportunity and adequate time for both parents to complete drug and alcohol treatment and regain the custody of their children.*

The Verdict (5)

Ask and you shall receive. Lawyers frequently fail to specifically ask for the relief they are seeking. This is a mistake. You must make a clear and concise request for the specific relief sough. This is typically the last statement you will make.

> *Your Honor, please issue your order immediately terminating the parental rights of John Doe and freeing Peter Doe for adoption.*

Rebuttal

Petitioner agency counsel is entitled to rebuttal following the respondents' closing argument. Some jurisdictions require that counsel reserve rebuttal opportunity prior to closing. If opposing closing argument accomplished nothing and the lawyer is confident the judge has received all-important information, rebuttal can and probably should be waived. Do not waive rebuttal before a jury.

Rebuttal should be very brief, perhaps fewer than five minutes. Rebuttal is restricted to the scope of opposing counsel's closing. Focus on rebutting any persuasive arguments made by opposing counsel, returning to the case theme, and making a final request for relief.

> *The respondent just asked you for yet another chance. The evidence showed so many chances the department gave this parent. When is enough, enough? When Janie is killed by her mother's boyfriend? Now is the time to give Janie a chance at a happy and healthy life. Please return the Verdict Form terminating the parent-child legal relationship.*

CHAPTER FOUR

CROSS-EXAMINATION
MINIMIZING AND MARGINALIZING WITNESS IMPACT

I'm finished with dis guy.

Vincent Gambini[1]

Take-Away

Minimize and marginalize the impact of direct with short, precise, factual statements.

Be firm, not rude.

Be realistic and cautious.

Get your closing facts and get out.

Minimize: to reduce or keep to a minimum.[2] Marginalize: to relegate to unimportant.[3] These are the goals of cross-examination. Winning the case is not a realistic goal of cross-examination. The witness, on cross, is not your witness and is not in court to prove your case. Attempts to use cross-examination to do so will likely backfire. It is wise to recognize that opposing witnesses are not present to help us— indeed they may be present to hurt us—and we should view cross-examination as an opportunity to minimize damage and marginalize the impact of the witness.

Cross-examination is difficult. It is an acquired skill, perhaps more than any other element of trial practice. Despite many a new litigators' proclamation that they "love" cross-examination, many experienced litigators and trial skills instructors tell us that cross-examination is usually the last skill to develop.

Cross-examination is dangerous. It typically involves on the one side a witness who presents facts and opinions damaging to your case, is frequently an advocate for the other side, and is likely to be in an oppositional mindset. The witness is not inclined to make the cross-examining lawyer's job of pulling out contrary testimony

---

1. From the film "My Cousin Vinnie" 20th Century Fox (1992). Street-wise New York City attorney Vincent Gambini, played by Joe Pesci, says this line after he has marginalized a key state's witness on cross-examination.

2. *Wikipedia.*

3. *Wikipedia.*

easy. Then enter that cross-examiner, frustrated from having listened to damaging testimony and anxious to quickly fix it all. The result is frequently an unpleasant exchange that the lawyer loses.

It is well said that one cannot win a case on cross, but one can lose it. It is imperative, therefore, that you recognize cross-examination for what it is: an opportunity to reduce the negative impact of direct examination, and not an opportunity to win one's case. When preparing cross-examination, therefore, err on the side of caution and realistic expectations.

Scope

According to Fed. R. Evid. 611(b), cross-examination should be limited to the subject matter, or scope, of direct examination. This is the general rule in U.S. jurisdictions, but some courts allow cross-examination to pursue any matter relevant to the proceedings and otherwise admissible. Where cross-examination is limited to the subject matter of direct, the cross-examiner may not inquire as to matters not raised on direct.

Exactly what is raised as subject matter on direct examination is subject to the interpretation of the court, and courts variously apply strict or more liberal approaches. Assume, for example, that the state's caseworker has testified to several but not all of the events reported in her investigation. A strict construction of the rule would limit the cross-examination to just those events discussed on direct. A more liberal, and probably more likely view, would be to allow inquiry as to all admissible matters contained as part of the investigation. An effective lawyer's headline introducing the cross-examination topic in such a case might be: "Ms. Caseworker, you have testified about three incidents that you included in your investigative report; I would like to talk to you now about a fourth incident that you included in the same report." Here, at a minimum, the attorney would be well positioned to make a good-faith argument that the inquiry is within the scope of direct examination.

Fed. R. Evid. 611(b) also provides that the credibility of a witness is always in issue and may be explored in cross-examination. In preparing for the cross of any particular witness, be sure to know well the witness's areas of bias, motive, and self-interest in the case. Such is almost always present and can be pointed out by a few pointed questions as one segment of the cross. One might ask of a physician, for example, "Doctor, of all one hundred child abuse cases in which you testified, you have never once testified that child abuse was appropriately founded." It is advisable in these situations to choose areas of credibility that are substantial and will not appear trivial or mean-spirited.

It is also well-recognized that an area of inquiry otherwise outside the scope of direct examination may be allowed because the witness (or his attorney) brings the matter out or "opens the door." Witnesses sometimes do this as part of an overly broad generalization in defense of or to promote themselves. For example, a parent might offer, not necessarily responsive to a question, that he or she never gets angry. This then would allow the cross-examiner to go into incidents of confrontations with teachers, employers, and caseworkers not mentioned on direct.

Strategy

Begin preparing for cross-examination by analyzing the impact of the direct examination. Ask two questions:

1. Did the direct examination negatively impact my case story? And if so,

2. Is there anything I can do about it?

Recall the theory and theme that comprise the story of this family. If the answer to the first question is clearly *no, the direct examination did not harm my case* (even though something unflattering may have come out) you should consider waiving cross. There is no requirement to cross-examine, and if one can honestly say that nothing is likely to be gained (or worse, that risk of loss is present) then waiver is justified. *Waiver* is also justified if the answer to the first question is *yes*, but the answer to the second question is *no*. If nothing can be done regarding damage inflicted, it may be best to simply let it be and not draw further attention to a case shortcoming.

Topic Selection

Topic selection for cross-examination is critical. While one area of cross is likely to be credibility and/or bias, you must be precise when selecting topics. You are ill advised to engage in an unfocused generalized attack on a witness's credibility. You should be armed with specific examples of relevant lack of credibility, bias, or case self-interest that can be communicated clearly and effectively.

In addition to credibility, you should choose one or more (some lawyers feel that more than three topics on cross is too many) substantive issues for cross-examination. Be cautious here not to simply rehash or restate points established in direct. Go somewhere very specific with the cross-examination topic. Additionally, guard against making cheap points on cross-examination that can be easily repaired and further developed on re-direct.

Topic areas typically fall within one or more of the following categories:

- Discredit the witness, as discussed in credibility and bias above.

- Discredit the testimony by eliciting additional facts or "the rest of the story."

- Elicit additional information that is harmful to the other side.

- Elicit additional information that helps prove your case (this is rare and is an exception to the general rule that cross should be focused on minimizing and marginalizing only).

Organize topics according to the principles of primacy and recency so that the strongest areas are addressed first and last, with weaker points in between.

Technique

Each point in cross-examination must be made clearly and completely.

- Introduce the topic.

- Focus on facts, not conclusions.

- Exhaust the factual inquiry.

- Stop before asking for the conclusion/jury argument.

- Move on to the next point.

The "Duck Technique" illustrates this method:

I'd like to talk to you about your testimony on direct examination where you denied being a duck.

Q: You live next to a lake, correct?

A: Yes.

Q: You swim in that lake.

A: Yes.

Q: You float on top of the water.

A: Yes.

Q: You paddle under the water with your feet.

A: Yes.

Q: You have webbed feet.

A: Yes.

Q: You have feathers.

A: Yes.

Q: You can fly.

A: Yes.

Q: But you can also walk.

A: Yes.

Q: And you waddle when you walk.

A: Yes.

Q: You have a beak, don't you?

A: Yes.

Q: And when you open your beak, you quack.

A: Yes.

Thank you. No further questions *or* **now let's talk about . . . .**

Silly though the duck example may seem, it illustrates important key strategies in cross-examination. The topic is clearly identified: previous testimony denying that he is a duck. The questions are factual: the physical characteristics of a duck. The topic has been sufficiently exhausted: pertinent physical characteristics have been identified. The examiner stops short of asking the witness to admit that which he will not admit: that he is a duck. That conclusion is saved for closing argument when the lawyer argues as follows:

> You heard the witness admit he waddles when he walks and that he quacks when he talks. Ladies and gentlemen, if it walks like a duck and it quacks like a duck, it's a duck!

> *Cross-examination questions are essentially declarative statements designed to produce a simple affirmation from the witness.*

Form

Cross-examination is the antithesis of direct examination. On direct examination, it is the attorney's job to highlight the witness and use open-ended questioning to prompt the storytelling that will allow the fact finder to identify with the witness; on cross, it is the attorney's job to limit the witness's testimony through confining, leading questions. It is appropriately said that cross-examination is about the lawyer, not the witness.

Leading Questions

Leading questions are the foundation of cross-examination. Cross-examination questions are, in fact, questions only in the sense that the witness may disagree with them. Cross-examination questions are essentially declarative statements designed to produce a simple affirmation from the witness.

Whereas a direct examination question is: *How many appointments did you miss?*, the cross-examination counterpart is: *You missed six appointments, correct?* A properly formed cross-examination leading question takes the fact in issue, states its existence to the witness, and instructs the witness to agree with the stated fact.

> *A properly formed cross-examination leading question takes the fact in issue, states its existence to the witness, and instructs the witness to agree with the stated fact.*

Recall the three levels of questions discussed in the direct examination chapter, this time with a witness on cross-examination who is disinclined to provide the sought after information:

1. Leading

   Q: The house was *filthy*, correct?

   A: Yes.

2. Suggesting

   Q: Was the house *filthy*?

   A: Well, maybe, not really filthy.

3. Open

   Q: What was the condition of the house?

A: It was OK; not perfect, but OK. I visit a lot of homes, and I'd say this parent was doing a pretty good job of housekeeping under the circumstances.

Clearly you must avoid question type "3" above. It is an invitation to the witness to tell her version of the fact at issue. Perhaps the worst mistake in this regard is to ask a "why" question on cross-examination because it encourages the witness to tell the most compelling version for her actions.

Likewise, avoid question type "2," even though it contains the answer and calls for a *yes* or *no* response. It nonetheless provides an opening for the witness to disagree and engage in explanation. Option number "1" is the correct form of the question on cross.

Headlines

Headlines are not just for direct examination. Headlines should also be used to organize your cross-examination, introduce topics, focus the witness and the fact finder, and transition from one area to the next. Attempts to trick the witness or "hide the ball" by disguising topic areas or bouncing from one area to another without headlines typically only succeed at confusing and annoying the fact finder.

Tag Lines

A tag line is that portion at the end of the leading question that essentially directs the witness to agree with the statement. The word *correct* is an effective tag line, as in: *You are the child's therapist, correct.* Tag lines should be used sparingly—primarily for special emphasis or where a witness requires prompting to respond.

Avoid tag lines such as *isn't that true (or correct)*, *is that not true*, *and are you not*, because they are confusing to the witness, the fact finder, and the appellate reviewer. It is not obvious whether the witness has agreed or disagreed if he answers affirmatively to the question: *You are the child's therapist, are you not?* Likewise, avoid prefacing a leading question with these same forms, as in: *Isn't it true that you are the child's therapist?*

It is acceptable and advisable to ask most if not all cross-examination questions without including a tag line. Instead, create an effective question by simply using the appropriate voice inflection when making a declarative statement—as in: *You are the child's therapist*—while making eye contact that communicates to the witness that the witness is being directed to respond affirmatively. Courts typically allow this technique, even over the occasional objection that there is no question pending. Where problems arise, simply ad the tag line.

Incremental Factual Questions

It is even more important to stick to the facts and to avoid opinions and conclusions on cross-examination than it is on direct. If a witness is inclined to disagree or argue with a question, that inclination is enhanced when the information concerns opinions and conclusions. A caseworker is unlikely to admit that she *dislikes* a parent, but can be forced to admit that she complained about the parent to a supervisor, tried to get transferred off the case, or argued with the parent and ended an interview early. The opinion or conclusion to be drawn from the facts can be saved and used at closing argument. The purpose of the examination is to establish the facts on which the closing arguments can be drawn.

Each cross-examination question should contain only one fact. Ask questions in incremental fashion so that each fact builds on the previous fact toward a point that is not asked and is saved for closing argument.

Let's talk about your job history.

Q: You are a plumber, correct?

A: Yes.

Q: You have held three jobs in the past twelve months.

A: Yes.

Q: Each of these has been a plumbing job.

A: Yes.

Let's address your job with Joe's Plumbing first.

Q: You started as an employee of Joe's Plumbing on February 15, 201__.

A: Yes.

Q: On that day you were sent to a job site.

A: Yes.

Q: You did not arrive at the job site.

A: That's right.

Q: Your employer spoke to you about that.

A: Right.

Q: He asked you what happened, correct?

A: Yes.

Q: You told him you got lost.

A: Yes.

Q: You worked for Joe's Plumbing for two weeks after that.

A: Yes.

Q: During those two weeks you missed work four times.

A: Yes.

Q: On March 1, 201_ you were fired.

Now let's go over your next job.

After detailing the firing from two more jobs in a brief period of time, thereby establishing facts that support a conclusion or opinion of incompetence and irresponsibility, to which the witness would never have agreed, the lawyer may make the following argument in closing:

> *Mr. Jones cannot provide for his children because he cannot keep a job. Despite a lucrative trade, his job history, by his own account, is a series of failures caused by his failure to bother to show up for work.*

Demeanor and Witness Control [4]

Witness control is imperative in cross-examination, and it is primarily a product of asking confining, leading questions based on facts with which the witness must agree.

To enhance witness control, the cross-examiner's demeanor and tone should be firm and direct. Direct eye contact further promotes witness control. The pace of questioning is also important. By starting with the most agreeable facts and building incrementally with short, staccato-like questions, you can establish a pattern of witness agreement.

> *Witness control is imperative in cross-examination, and it is primarily a product of asking confining leading questions based on facts to which the witness must agree.*

---

4. *See also* chapter six, Difficult Witnesses: Managing the Challenge.

Cross-examination need not be cross. Cross-examination is not an invitation to engage in a fight with the witness. Angry exchanges between the witness and lawyer tend to offend the listeners (including your fact finders), are uncomfortable to watch, cause the witness to become more disagreeable, and overshadow any measurable points made. While there will be occasions when you must "get tough" with a witness, those situations must be warranted and your toughness must be seen as appropriate in response to the circumstances. It is a good rule of thumb to begin every cross-examination with a calm, business-like demeanor. And don't forget, you have a charge to conduct all courtroom activity in a professional manner.

Cross-Examination Answer/Impeachment Chart

Witness: **Jane Watson, MA, Case Worker**

Fact	Source	Date	Page	Line
MA in Fine Arts, not MSW	CV		1	10
Employed 8 Months Ago	CV		2	6
No Previous CW Experience	CV			
Prior Contact Unfounded	Inv. Rpt.	1-23-201_	1	22
Mother "Very Difficult"	Contact Rpt.	5-1-201_	1	16
"Well Adjusted Child"	Contact Rpt.	5-3-201_	5	11
Both Parents " Cooperative"	Contact Rpt.	5-5-201_	4	13
Not "Concerned" About Siblings	Rept. To Ct.	7-11-201_	13	27

The Answer/Impeachment[5] Chart

It is well established that a lawyer shall not ask a cross-examination question to which she does not know the answer. It is imperative, therefore, for witness control and impeachment, that the lawyer has quick access to the precise location of the sought answer in the record. You should prepare an Impeachment/Answer Chart containing, at a minimum, the information and location for each potentially difficult-to-elicit fact sought.

Recross-Examination

Recross-examination may be allowed at the court's discretion.[6] Recross is limited in scope to the redirect that preceded it. The decision to recross should be based on the same analysis as was the decision to cross: did the redirect harm my case and can I do anything to repair it? Both components of the analysis must be answered affirmatively in order to recross.

---

5. *See also* chapter six, Difficult Witnesses: Managing the Challenge, for a complete discussion of impeachment.
6. FED. R. EVID. 611.

CHAPTER FIVE

EXPERT WITNESS EXAMINATION
MOVING FROM PERCEPTION TO BELIEF

Q: *Doctor, please tell us what happened to this child.*

A: *Someone shook her to death.*[1]

Take-Away

Elicit a compelling opinion through eight phases of expert exam:

1. *Introduction*

2. *Context*

3. *Accreditation*

4. *Tender*

5. *Opinion*

6. *Assignment*

7. *Basis*

8. *Persuasion*

Cross-examine with caution as to bias and assumptions, not conclusions.

Expert testimony is critically important in child welfare cases. Child Welfare Court experts influence whether a child is determined to be abused or neglected in the adjudication phase, which placements are in a child's best interests in the disposition phase, and whether the parent-child relationship should end in the termination phase. Using experts effectively is an essential skill of the child welfare lawyer.

Expert testimony is a bright-line exception to the rule that a witness must testify based on perception. Lay or fact witnesses must testify (with very limited exception for lay witness opinion) about what the witness perceived through the senses. This is not true for an expert. An expert witness may testify to *opinion*; in other words, an expert witness may testify about what the expert *believes*. In child welfare court,

---

1. An expert opinion in a Shaken Baby Syndrome case.

expert beliefs frequently take the form of the causes and consequences of human behavior and conditions. Such opinions may be based on observation and interaction with the parties or simply on information gathered and reviewed while preparing to give an expert opinion. Because an expert's belief is based on special knowledge the average fact finder does not possess, the effect is a disproportionately heavy influence on what the fact finder will believe.

Child welfare court experts typically testify whether a child was abused, how a child was abused, the effects of abuse or neglect (including the current and long-term medical and mental health impact), the parents' capacity to parent adequately, and the best interests of the child. Mental health experts may testify as to mental health disorders and diagnoses. An expert may even testify as to the ultimate issue in the case.[2]

Experts may also testify as to syndrome evidence. This is particularly important in child welfare cases that involve Battered Child Syndrome, Shaken Baby Syndrome, Parental Alienation Syndrome, Child Sexual Abuse Accommodation Syndrome, and Munchausen Syndrome by Proxy.

Attorneys are limited through the course of trial in their ability to submit isolated, persuasive, conclusive information to the court. Expert testimony provides such an opportunity. It is difficult to justify failing to call expert witnesses in a child abuse, neglect, or dependency case.

The Law of Expert Witness Examination

Admissibility

The child welfare lawyer should consult applicable federal and state law and commentary to determine the rules of expert testimony in your jurisdiction. Federal Rule of Evidence 702 provides the following traditional, threshold, two-prong test for the admission of expert testimony:

The Helpfulness Rule

Will the scientific, technical, or other specialized knowledge assist the trier of fact in a) understanding evidence, or b) determining a fact in issue? Courts have traditionally used a common sense test for helpfulness, asking whether the information is commonly known or understood.[3]

---

2. FED. R. EVID. 704.

3. U.S. v. Mulder, 273 F.3d 91, 102 (2d Cir. 2001).

The Qualification Rule

Does the witness possess "sufficient" scientific, technical, or other specialized knowledge to testify about such information? Sufficiency is established by showing any or a combination of the following: knowledge, skill, experience, training, or education. Sufficiency does not require a showing that the expert is outstanding, well known, or respected.[4]

Following the U.S. Supreme Court decisions in *Daubert*[5] and *Kumho*,[6] Fed. R. Evid. 702 was amended in 2000 to add a third admission test[7] to the threshold two-part test above. The so-called *Daubert* test is applied in federal court and some state courts, typically on a challenge that the proposed expert testimony is novel and not sufficiently reliable. In such cases, the court may hold a *Daubert* hearing. This could occur in child welfare cases where new or controversial syndrome evidence is proposed.

The *Daubert* Rule

Is the information that the expert proposes to give reliable or trustworthy in an evidentiary sense? In this "gatekeeper" function, the court determines whether a) the testimony is based on sufficient data, b) is the product of reliable principles and methods, and c) the expert has applied these principles and methods reliably.[8]

Basis

Expert testimony may be based on a wide range of information known by the expert. The factual basis or foundation in data for the expert opinion is persuasive but not required.[9] The basis for testimony may include firsthand knowledge, such as that which a treating emergency room physician may have. Basis may also be a records review by a physician who has never seen the child patient.

Additionally, experts may give opinions based on information that is not admissible so long as it is of the type of evidence reasonably relied on by experts in forming such opinions.[10] This includes hearsay statements. For example, an expert physician could rely on a neighbor's hearsay statement about a child's abuse as part of

---

4. FED. R. EVID. 702, Commentary.
5. Daubert v. Merrell Dow Pharmaceuticals, Inc., 509 U.S. 579 (1993).
6. Kumho Tire Co. v. Carmichael, 26 U.S. 137 (1999).
7. Some states have not incorporated this part of the federal rule and may instead treat the issue as a matter of weight rather than admissibility.
8. FED. R. EVID. 702, Committee Note (2000).
9. FED. R. EVID. 705.
10. *Id.*

the diagnostic history. Such relied-on statements, are not, however, generally admissible themselves.

The Certainty Standard

Law and convention in some jurisdictions require an expert witness opinion certainty standard. This standard requires that the expert testify, before or after the opinion is given, that the opinion is held to a degree of certainty. The most commonly used standard is "reasonable degree of professional certainty." Lawyers should, in such jurisdictions, simply ask the experts whether they hold the opinion to a reasonable degree of certainty within their profession. Alternately, the lawyer may insert the specific profession, by asking, for example, whether the opinion is held to a reasonable degree of medical certainty.

Court-Appointed Experts

Fed. R. Evid. 706 provides that the court may, on its own motion or a party's motion, appoint an expert or experts. The court may take nominations from the parties, the parties may stipulate to an expert, or the court may appoint one of its own choosing. Such court-appointed experts are to be advised of their duties, shall be reasonably compensated, and the court may order the parties to provide compensation. The court or any party may call the expert to testify. The expert is subject to cross-examination, even by the party calling the expert. The court appointment of an expert does not limit the parties from calling their own experts.

Expert Witness Direct Examination

Use Direct Examination Basics

Expert witness direct is direct examination *supersized*. Expert direct includes everything one receives with lay witness direct, plus a persuasive, authoritative opinion. Do not abandon the general rules of direct examination for an expert. Use them for the same reason they are useful in lay witness examination—persuasion. In particular, remember to:

- Tie expert testimony to case theory and theme.

- Prepare the witness.

- Focus the examination on the witness.

- Humanize the witness.

- Use nonleading, open-ended questions for nonfoundational matters.

- Use leading or suggesting questions for foundational matters.

- Use headlines, transitions, and loopbacks.

- Use visual aids.

- Use the principles of primacy and recency with multiple opinions or bases.

- Avoid long narratives.

- Establish primacy over opposing expert.

- Break up testimony and enumerate lists.

- Use teaching examples and analogies.

- Evaluate the need for or amount of redirect dispassionately.

Organization

Expert examination is typically detailed and complex. It requires skillful organization to be understandable and persuasive. Whereas lay witness direct examination is organized across three sections (introducing and accrediting the witness, setting the scene, and describing the action), these sections are developed and expanded into the following eight distinct sections for expert examination. By using these eight sections, you can not only make preparing the expert witness examination manageable, you can also make its execution more effective.

1. Introduction

2. Context

3. Accreditation

4. Tender

5. Opinion

6. Assignment

7. Basis (including methodology)

8. Persuasion

1. Introduction

Introduce the witness briefly.

Good morning, Doctor.

Q: Please tell us your name.

A: I am Dr. Robert Kiley.

Q: What kind of doctor are you?

Q: A: I am a pediatric neurologist.

Q: What is a pediatric neurologist?

A: A pediatric neurologist is a medical doctor who specializes in the treatment of children who suffer from disorders of the central nervous system, including brain injuries.

Q: Where do you work, Doctor?

A: Here in Nita City, at Nita University Hospital and Medical School.

Q: What is your position?

A: I am Chief of Pediatric Neurology and Professor of Medicine.

2. Context

Foreshadow why the doctor is present—i.e., to give a specific opinion. Do not elicit the opinion yet; an adequate foundation has not been laid. Ask precise, primarily leading, foundational questions.

Doctor, I want to talk to you about why you are here today.

Q: Have you been retained to review the medical condition of little Mary Ellen?

A: Yes.

Q: Have you done this?

A: Yes.

Q: Have you also been retained to give an expert opinion on the cause of Mary Ellen's injury?

A: Yes.

Q: Have you formed such an opinion?

A: Yes.

Q: Are you prepared to give that opinion today?

A: Yes.

Doctor, before you may give that opinion, I must ask you some questions about your qualifications to do so.

A: I understand.

3. Accreditation

Accreditation is the means by which the foundation for the opinion is laid. It is more than a formality. Accreditation not only establishes the Rule 702 criteria for admission of the opinion, it also persuades the finder of fact of the validity and weight of the expert opinion. Accreditation should be interesting, persuasive, and tied to the specific opinion elicited immediately following accreditation. Do not stipulate to the experts qualifications. Likewise, respond to any objections that accreditation is wasting the court's time by explaining that you are required to make a record of the expert's qualifications and that such qualifications are important and go to the weight of the testimony and opinion.

It is unpersuasive and objectionable to ask the witness to simply describe his or her qualifications. It is the lawyer's job to organize and highlight those qualifications. Likewise, it is ineffective to merely "walk" the listener through a resume or curriculum vitae (CV). Much of the information in a CV is not relevant to the opinion, and it is boring. Do not attempt to introduce the CV. It is hearsay. Additionally, if admitted, the expert's qualification testimony can be excluded as cumulative. At a minimum, be certain that the expert testifies about her education and/or experience. Remember to humanize the expert; she should not be viewed by the fact finder as a computer. Customary expert accreditation headline topics include the following:

- Education

- Training

- Licensure / Certification / Professional Associations

- Experience

- Teaching / Lecturing / Continuing Education

- Publications

- Prior Expert Testimony

Doctor, let's begin by covering your education and training.

Q: What college degrees do you hold?

A: I have a bachelor of science with high honors in biology from Georgetown University.

Q: What advanced or professional degree do you hold?

A: I received a medical degree, an MD, from Nita University with high honors.

Q: When did you receive your medical degree?

A: 1990.

Q: How long have you practiced medicine, Doctor?

A: Since I graduated twenty-one years ago.

Q: What special training did you receive as you began practicing medicine?

A: I did my residency at Yale University Hospital in pediatric neurology.

Q: What is a residency?

A: It is a period of intensive on-the-job training that a doctor completes in his or her specialty.

Q: What other special training did you receive?

A: I did a fellowship in pediatric neurology at Colorado University.

Q: What is a fellowship?

A: It is a post-doctoral, extra if you will, training period in one's specialty.

Q: Do most doctors do a fellowship?

A: No. It is reserved for selected applicants and is highly selective.

Doctor, let's move to your licensing.

Q: Are you licensed to practice medicine?

A: Yes, I hold a license to practice medicine here in the state of Nita.

Q: Do you hold any board certifications?

A: Yes, three. I am board certified in pediatric medicine, neurology, and pediatric neurology.

Q: Please explain to us what board certification is.

A: Board certification is the process a doctor can go through to establish him or herself as proficient in a specialty. One trains and then must pass an exam. You must also stay current and update your certifications periodically.

Q: As a result of your board certifications, do you have special admitting privileges at any hospitals?

A: Yes. I have admitting privileges in all hospitals in Nita City.

You said earlier that you have practiced medicine for twenty-one years; I'd like to discuss that experience now.

Q: *You said you started your training with your residency and then fellowship at Yale and Colorado Universities; why?*

A: They selected me, and I wanted to be trained by the best. Yale and CU are premier institutions for the study and practice of pediatric neurology.

Q: What was the focus of your work at that time?

A: We would diagnose and treat children with head trauma.

Q: What did you do after your fellowship?

A: I was offered a position here, back home, in pediatric neurology, at Nita University Hospital; I took it and have been here ever since.

Q: And what has been the focus of your work at Nita University hospital?

A: The same thing: the diagnosis and treatment of children with head trauma.

Q: Please describe what your work is like.

A: It is very intense. Children are in very dangerous positions that frequently involve life or death or long-term disability. Head injuries and brain trauma can be deceptive, and the response must be prompt.

Q: What are the typical causes of brain trauma in children?

A: They are not naturally occurring so they are caused either by blunt force trauma or the shaking of a child.

Q: Do you determine the cause?

A: Yes.

Q: Why?

A: Because we are asked to by law enforcement and because cause and treatment are connected. If we know the cause, we can better treat the injury.

You mentioned shaking could cause brain injury, let's talk about that just a little now and in more detail later.

Q: How does this occur?

A: It is called Shaken Baby Syndrome, and it occurs when someone shakes a child aggressively, causing the head to whiplash and the brain to move inside the skull.

Q: How many shaken baby cases have you diagnosed or treated?

A: Approximately 350.

Doctor, you mentioned earlier that you are a professor, let's talk about your teaching position.

Q: What is that position?

A: I am a Professor of Medicine at Nita University Medical School.

Q: What do you teach?

A: Pediatric medicine, neurology, and medical ethics.

Q: And what is your primary teaching focus?

A: Pediatric neurology, specifically children's brain injuries.

Q: Does that include the diagnosis and treatment of Shaken Baby Syndrome?

A: Yes.

Q: How long have you been teaching?

A: Fifteen years.

Let's move now to your writing credentials.

Q: Do you publish material on your medical specialty?

A: Yes, I have published numerous articles and book chapters within my specialty.

Q: Can you name any that relate specifically to this case?

A: Yes, my most recent article is called "The Science of Shaken Baby Syndrome."

Q: Where was this article published?

A: JAMA, the Journal of the American Medical Association.

Q: Is that a peer-reviewed publication?

A: Yes.

Q: What does peer review mean?

A: It means it is not published without professional scrutiny. The proposed article must be reviewed by the experts in the field for approval.

Q: What did this article cover?

A: It is a comprehensive review of the state of the science of Shaken Baby Syndrome, including causes, consequences, frequency, diagnoses, and treatment.

Q: Did you use scientific data in this article?

A: Yes, we used the results of our five-year study of shaken baby cases conducted here at Nita University Hospital.

Finally, Doctor, let's talk about your previous experience as an expert witness.

Q: Have you testified as an expert witness in court before?

A: Yes, many times.

Q: In what field were you qualified as an expert?

A: Pediatric neurology, with an emphasis in brain injury.

Thank you, Dr. Kiley.

4. Tender

Tender the witness as an expert in a field sufficient to allow the expert testimony you seek, including the expert opinion(s). Be specific so that it is clear that an expert so designated would be qualified to give the opinion you seek. Be broad enough to allow the expert to testify as to all expert material you seek. Some jurisdictions do not tender the witness.

> Your Honor, pursuant to Rule 702 and the doctor's special education and training, I tender Dr. Kiley as an expert witness in Pediatric Neurology with an emphasis in brain injuries.

At this point, the court will ask whether opposing counsel has any objection. Assuming no objection or that the objection is overruled, the court will accept the witness as an expert as designated. This is also the opportunity for opposing counsel to voir dire the witness regarding qualifications. Such voir dire may disqualify a witness or simply point out some weakness in background that can go to weight. Voir dire may be followed by an objection as to expertise or no objection.

5. Opinion

The opinion is the reason the expert witness is called to testify. It should be powerful, clear, and concise. Above all, get the expert opinion. Ask for a specific opinion as to a specific matter. For example, it is vague and objectionable to ask merely, "what is your opinion?" Instead, for example, ask: "What is your opinion as to the cause of death?"

The fact finder has been waiting to hear the opinion from the outset of the testimony. Everything done to this point has been in anticipation of this moment. You won't be overdoing it by being a bit dramatic here in terms of word choice and voice inflection. Remember to ask for the level of professional certainty in jurisdictions where this is required.

> **Doctor, I am now going to ask you for your expert opinions on two issues.**
>
> Q: Doctor, do you have an opinion as to Mary Ellen's current condition?
>
> A: Yes.
>
> Q: What is that opinion?
>
> A: Mary Ellen has suffered severe and permanent brain damage.
>
> Q: Do you hold this opinion to a reasonable degree of medical certainty?
>
> A: Yes.
>
> Q: Doctor, do you also have an opinion as to the cause of Mary Ellen's permanent and severe brain damage?

A: Yes, I do.

Q: What is that opinion?

A: Mary Ellen's injuries are the result of being shaken violently, also called Shaken Baby Syndrome.

Q: Do you hold this opinion to a reasonable degree of medical certainty?

A: Yes, I do.

6. Assignment

The assignment stage is the opportunity to clarify what the expert was hired to do, dispel any notion that the expert's relationship and fee are inappropriate, and set up an explanation for the basis and methodology for the opinion(s).

Dr. Kiley, I want to talk next about how you formed your expert opinions, beginning with what you were hired to determine.

Q: Have you been retained by the Nita Department of Family Services to help determine what happened to Mary Ellen?

A: Yes.

Q: Are you being compensated for this?

A: Yes.

Q: Is your compensation the regular fee for expert physician services in pediatric neurology?

A: Yes.

Q: What, then, was your assignment in this case?

A: I was hired to do three things: (1) diagnose Mary Ellen's condition, (2) give a prognosis for her recovery, and (3) make a determination of the cause of the condition.

Q: Did you do each of those three things?

A: Yes.

7. Basis (including methodology)

The basis phase of the examination provides the opportunity to support the expert opinion(s) by showing the soundness of the expert's information and process.

Let's talk now about how you completed your assignment.

Q: What information did you use to reach your opinions?

A: I used three kinds of information, or what we call data sets. First, I reviewed the complete record or case history for Mary Ellen. Second, I performed a comprehensive examination of Mary Ellen. Third, I assessed the information I gathered in steps one and two against the existing scientific and medical scholarship.

Q: Why did you choose to do those things?

A: These are the accepted methods in our field for forming a reliable expert opinion.

Q: What process or methodology did you then use to form your opinion from this data?

A: I used the scientific method. I took the questions posed to me, collected the data, formed a hypothesis or probable diagnosis, tested that diagnosis for consistency or inconsistency, and when the data and the diagnosis were entirely consistent, I formed my opinion.

Q: Why did you approach your work in that way?

A: That is the accepted methodology within our profession.

8. Persuasion

Persuasion, also called explanation or teaching, is the final phase of expert examination and the opportunity to persuade the fact finder of the validity of the expert opinion. This is done through a series of questions and answers that allow the witness to explain why the opinion is valid and why the opposing opinion is invalid. It is an opportunity for the witness to teach the fact finder some of the scientific or technical information relied on. This phase can be lengthy, relative to the other sections, although it should remain interesting. It should anticipate both cross-examination and the opposing expert opinion by covering the expert's assumptions and by using theory differentiation. This section should be organized so that the expert repeats his opinions and ends on the strongest point. (The following illustration is highly abbreviated and covers only one of the sample expert's opinions.)

Doctor, I would like to talk to you now about your opinion that *Mary Ellen's injuries are the result of Shaken Baby Syndrome.*

Q: Why did you conclude that Mary Ellen suffered from Shaken Baby Syndrome?

A: Because all of my data from both the medical history and examination are consistent with Shaken Baby Syndrome and no other cause.

Q: Let's start with the data from the medical history; how was it consistent with Shaken Baby Syndrome?

A: Several ways. The most compelling piece of data that points directly to Shaken Baby Syndrome is the skull CT scan taken by the on-staff radiologist when Mary Ellen was brought into Emergency. It shows clear signs of a brain injury caused by shaking.

Q: Doctor, using exhibit 1, the CT scan you referenced, please explain to us how it shows brain injury caused by shaking.

Your Honor, may Dr. Kiley step down and use the CT scan display unit to explain his testimony?

A: This image shows the brain inside the skull. This area here, labeled "B," shows extensive subdural hematoma or bleeding inside the skull. And this section here, labeled "S," shows swelling of the brain. Both of these are highly indicative of serious brain injury and Shaken Baby Syndrome.

Q: Could those things have been caused by something other than shaking?

A: In theory, yes, but that's why you use multiple data sources. Here, with Mary Ellen, no other cause is plausible because there was no evidence of blunt force trauma to the skull from the outside.

Q: Why does that matter?

A: Because the only other plausible explanation for the bleeding is blunt force trauma to the skull, and there was none—no skull fracture, no impact marks, no bruising, no cuts or bleeding.

Q: Did the records indicate an explanation for the injury from the parents?

A: Yes, the records indicate the parents told medical staff the child had rolled off the couch onto her head.

Q: Is that plausible?

A: No. Such a fall could not have caused these injuries.

Q: Are explanations like the one given by the parents in this case also important to your diagnosis?

A: Yes, highly inconsistent explanations, or what doctors call history, are indicators of inflicted abuse.

Doctor, let's move on now to Dr. Burns's opinion in this case.

Q: Do you know Dr. Burns?

A: Yes.

Q: How do you know him?

A: He regularly testifies for parent's accused of shaking their children, and he performed a records review in this case.

Q: Are you familiar with Dr. Burns's opinion in this case?

A: Yes, he concluded the injuries could have been accidental and caused by the fall the parents described.

Q: Do you agree with his opinion?

A: Absolutely not.

Q: Why not?

A: Because it is not credible, is not supported by the data, and ignores the established science in this field.

Q: Having reviewed Dr. Burns's work, does it alter your opinion in any way?

A: No. To the contrary, it is clear that this child was shaken violently and that that caused her brain damage.

Q: Will Mary Ellen recover from this, Doctor?

A: No, she is permanently brain damaged.

Thank you, Doctor.

Expert Witness Cross-Examination

Cross-examination is inherently dangerous; cross-examining an expert witness magnifies that danger. Do not fence with Zorro. You will lose.

Still, there is much that can be done to minimize or marginalize an expert witness. The keys to expert witness cross-examination are precise questioning and reasonable expectations. Apply the general rules of cross-examination. As to form, the focus must be on the lawyer, and all questions must be leading and controlling. Topically, do not attack the expert's opinion directly. Experts do not change their opinions on the stand. Experts are, however, vulnerable in four distinct areas: their credibility and bias, cross-expert validation, limitation of assignment, and their assumptions and methodology.

Credibility and Bias

Fees

It can be effective to expose exorbitant fees. The mere fact that a witness is being compensated is not generally an effective showing of bias and can appear as a petty attack.

> **Let's talk about your fees.**
>
> Q: Your standard fee for services is $200 per hour?
>
> A: Yes.
>
> Q: But you are being paid more than that for your expert services now?
>
> A: Yes.
>
> Q: You are being paid $300 per hour for witness services for preparing your opinion.
>
> A: Yes.
>
> Q: And you are being paid $400 per hour for your in-court time.
>
> A: Yes.

Ideology

Experts are sometimes aligned with a particular cause or faction within a professional discipline. Showing that a witness always testifies for child protective services or is known to be pro-"family preservation" can be effective to show bias through self-interest.

Let's talk about your views on child protection.

Q: You belong to an organization called Parent's Unite?

A: Yes.

Q: Parent's Unite believes children are wrongly removed from their parents by the government?

A: Sometimes, yes.

Q: You share that view, correct?

A: Yes.

Credentials

While an expert may qualify to give an opinion under the rules, the weight of the opinion can be lessened by showing weakness in educational or experiential credentials. A family practitioner or internist may render an opinion on child maltreatment that is less persuasive than the opinion coming from the pediatrician who is board certified in child abuse.

Let's talk about your qualifications.

Q: You are not board certified in pediatrics?

A: Correct.

Q: You practice family medicine?

A: Yes.

Q: You do not regularly treat child abuse victims, correct?

A: Correct.

Q: Your medical practice involves such things as adult diabetes?

A: Yes.

Q: Colds and flu?

A: Yes.

Cross-Expert Validation

Have the opposing expert validate your expert where possible. One expert may recognize the other expert as an authority in the field. Additionally, establish where there are substantive areas of agreement.

> Let's talk about your colleague, Dr. Smith.

Q: You are familiar with Dr. Smith's work?

A: Yes.

Q: You have read her article on pediatric burn injuries?

A: Yes.

Q: You recognize Dr. Smith as an authority in burn injuries?

A: Yes.

Q: You reviewed Dr. Smith's expert report in this case?

A: Yes.

Q: And you don't dispute the soundness of her report methodology.

A: No, I don't.

Limitation of Assignment and Scope of Opinion

Assignment Limits

Clarify the limitations of the opposing expert's assignment. The fact finder should not apply the expert's opinion more broadly than is appropriate. An expert retained to render an opinion only about a parent's mental health should not be allowed to render, even implicitly, an opinion on the placement of children. Clarify that the expert has no opinion as to a certain matter.

> Doctor, I want to return to your assignment in this case.

Q: You were hired to assess Ms. Jones's mental health, correct?

A: Correct.

Q: And you did that?

A: Correct.

Q: You were not hired to give a custody recommendation?

A: Right.

Q: You did not meet with the children?

A: Correct.

Q: You did not observe the children interact with their mother?

A: Correct.

Q: You do not have an opinion on the placement of the children?

A: Correct.

Scope of Opinion

Similarly, the same expert, retained to render an opinion on a parent's mental health, must not be permitted to render an opinion about custody if inclined to do so. Object to any attempts to do so. If that objection is overruled, use cross-examination to show how the opinion exceeds the scope of the assignment and the expert's authority.

What the Expert Did Not Do

That which the expert did not do or did not devote substantial time and resources to is a rich area for cross-examination. Failure to do that which a reasonable person would expect diminishes an expert's opinion.

Let's discuss your fieldwork in this case.

Q: You performed a parent-child interaction assessment?

A: Yes.

Q: You performed twenty hours of interviews and observations?

A: Yes.

Q: And only two hours of that time were spent observing the parents and children together?

A: Yes.

Q: That's 10 percent of the total time.

A: I suppose.

Q: Your parent-child interaction assessment involved only 10 percent parent-child interaction.

A: Yes.

Q: You did not meet with the children's grandparents?

A: No.

Q: Teachers?

A: No.

Q: Foster parents?

A: No.

Q: Neighbors?

A: No.

Assumptions and Methodology

Misplaced reliance on statements, data, theories, and scholarship is the basis for flawed assumptions and methodology cross-examination. If the expert's "math is wrong," it will follow that the opinion is unreliable. Experts must agree that where an assumption is changed, the outcome can or would change. Likewise, flawed methodology produces unreliable results.

Experts rely on witness statements, prior testimony, and data provided to them. Where the data can be shown to be flawed, it follows that the opinion derived therefrom is also flawed. Show where an expert relied on outdated, suspect, or controversial theories. Use learned treatises and other authoritative scholarship to show that an expert's findings or methodology are inconsistent with accepted norms.

> **Doctor, I would like to discuss certain assumptions you made in forming your opinion.**
>
> Q: You concluded that the hot-water burn injury to the child's hand was the result of intentional abuse?
>
> A: Correct.
>
> Q: You concluded that the child's hand was forcibly held in the hot water?
>
> A: Yes.
>
> Q: And you made certain assumptions in forming that opinion?
>
> A: Yes.
>
> Q: One such assumption that you made was that the temperature of the water was between 115 and 120 degrees.
>
> A: Correct.

Q: Because at such a temperature, the child's hand would have to be in the water for an extended period in order to burn?

A: Yes.

Q: And it is unlikely the child would have held his hand in the water that long by himself?

A: Correct.

Q: So the water temperature assumption is key to your conclusion?

A: Yes.

Q: If the water temperature were significantly higher, your opinion might be different.

A: It's possible.

Well, let's talk about that possibility.

Q: A hot water temperature of 150 degrees would burn a child's hand quickly, correct?

A: Yes.

Q: At 150 degrees, a child's hand could burn in one to two seconds?

A: Yes.

Q: And such an injury could be accidental?

A: Yes.

Q: Doctor, you did not test the water temperature at this child's apartment did you?

A: No.

Q: You relied on the statement of the landlord that the temperature was approximately 120 degrees?

A: Yes.

Q: That is an assumption you made?

A: Yes.

Q: That is what the landlord told the police.

A: That's my understanding.

Q: 150 degrees would be an unsafe temperature to keep water at around a small child?

A: True.

Q: You don't know whether the landlord told the police the truth?

A: No, I don't; I assume he did.

Q: You accepted the assumption that the water was 120 degrees.

A: I did make that assumption.

Q: And if your assumption is incorrect, your conclusion could be incorrect?

A: It's possible.

Q: Because at 150 degrees, this child's injury could have been an accident.

A: I suppose that's true.

No further questions.

CHAPTER SIX

DIFFICULT WITNESSES
MANAGING THE CHALLENGE

Yeahbut[1]

Take-Away

Anticipate, avoid, remain poised, exercise control techniques, impeach, refresh, and move along.

It is not a question of *if*, it is a question of *when*. Witnesses *will* be difficult, and *when* we have difficult witnesses, our job is to be unsurprised and manage the challenge. Preparation, organization, question form, and question substance, are keys to avoiding examination problems. In other words, good questions get good answers.[2] When problems do arise, the lawyer can use certain questioning techniques to control the problem witness. When witnesses forget, we can refresh recollection. Impeachment can be used to force a difficult witness to acknowledge an inconsistent statement.

It is imperative to retain one's composure and professionalism when dealing with a difficult witness. Judges and juries are typically offended when lawyers quarrel with witnesses. You are well advised to remember that managing difficult witnesses is merely part of the job of the trial lawyer. Bad witness behavior will reflect badly on the witness, and lawyers should be mindful to not take the behavior personally. If anticipated and managed, witness difficulty need not be a crisis and can instead be an opportunity to better advocate for the client.

Good Questions Get Good Answers

Witness difficulty typically arises on cross-examination, but can occur with our own witnesses on direct examination as well. In both instances, the better the question, the better the chance of getting a good answer. Lawyers should be willing to

---

1. Definition: an answer in agreement but with a condition, as in "Yeahbut he started it." Plural as in, "that witness has a bad case of the yeahbuts." Attribution goes to NITA President, John Baker, Esq., for his work in identifying and managing witness yeahbuts in trial skills training.
2. Attribution goes to NITA Program Director Mark Caldwell for identifying this maxim.

test their questions against good questioning technique to increase the likelihood of a successful examination.

Difficult Witness Direct Examination Question Review

1. Is the witness adequately prepared such that the witness knows the question topics, order, organization, and form of the question?

2. Are headlines, transitions, and loopbacks used to direct the witness to the area of questioning?

3. Do the questions proceed in an incremental, linear time sequence?

4. Is the question limited to one piece of information?

5. Does the question call for a fact and not a conclusion (except for rare lay witness opinion or expert opinions)?

6. Does this witness know the information from the witness's own experience and personal knowledge; i.e., does adequate foundation exist?

Difficult Witness Cross-Examination Question Review

1. Do I know the answer?

2. Must the witness answer as I wish?

3. Do I know precisely where the answer is found in the record for impeachment purposes?

4. Is the question adequately leading; that is, is the question really a declarative statement to which I am directing the witness to agree?

5. Is the question short?

6. Does the question call for only one piece of data?

7. Does the question call for a fact and not a conclusion (except for rare lay witness opinion or expert opinions)?

8. Is the examination organization logical, fair, and understandable?

Techniques for Cross-Examination Witness Control

Get Agreement and Establish Pace Early

It is important to establish a pattern of witness agreement early. Witnesses who become accustomed to agreeing with the cross-examining lawyer early tend to continue to do so. Begin the examination not with confrontation, but with a collegial demeanor and questions with which it is easy for the witness to agree. Establish an efficient pace with short, clear, and simple statements that are unlikely to draw resistance from the witness.

Establish and Maintain Authority

The witness should feel that the cross-examining attorney is the authority figure in the attorney-witness relationship. While you should not be cross or hostile, you should establish and maintain an authoritative position. Be firm with the witness— use posture, voice volume, voice inflection, and direct eye contact. Avoid ending the question (declarative statement) on an "uptick" of voice inflection. In other words, the question must not sound like a question.

Managing Nonresponsive and Self-Serving Answers

Witnesses will frequently respond to cross-examination questions by deflecting the question to make their own advocacy point on the subject raised. A witness may answer, "Yes, but . . .," or simply avoid the question altogether and begin testifying as to the point the witness wishes to make.

Q: You missed five appointments, correct?

A: Yes, but I called first, and I told Ms. Worker the week before that I couldn't come on Tuesdays, and she was not being fair to me.

In these circumstances, the following techniques can be used:

The "Your Answer Is . . ." Technique

After the witness is finished, simply state back to the witness: "The answer to my question is *yes*?" Witnesses will frequently state "yes," and the lawyer has the answer. After doing this several times, witnesses will frequently conform to the process and begin answering with a simple "yes."

The Re-Ask Technique

After the witness is finished, simple re-ask the question by stating: "My question is . . . ."

Move to Strike

When the nonresponsive answer is too damaging to leave on the record, or the witness is consistently nonresponsive, move to strike the nonresponsive answer: "Objection, nonresponsive, move to strike everything after the word 'yes.'"

The Reason-with-the-Witness Technique

Lawyers will, on occasion, attempt to gain witness control by asking for the witness's cooperation. This is not a preferred technique by many lawyers. Still, the lawyer may say:

> "Please simply answer my question."

> "It is important that you answer the question I ask."

> "You can talk about that when your attorney asks you questions. For now, please just answer my question."

Raise the Hand of God (aka, The Stop Sign)

Nonresponsive answers can sometimes be controlled by signaling to the witness that he should stop talking immediately by raising one's hand in the fashion by which a police officer stops traffic. Be aware that efforts to cut off a witness can cause an unwanted confrontation, so manage this technique carefully. Never interrupt a witness by yelling over them.

The Ask-Mom-for-Help Technique

The judge has the authority to control the manner of examination under Fed. R. Evid. 611(a). As such, it is permissible to ask the judge for assistance in controlling the witness. Lawyers may ask: "Your Honor, will you please instruct the witness to answer the question?" Some lawyers and trial skills instructors see this as a last resort, if not an admission of weakness by the lawyer. Judges may do as requested, particularly if the witness has been uncooperative for an extended period. Some judges may advise counsel that the witness is the lawyer's responsibility, not theirs.

Be "Diplomatic"

It will, on occasion, be necessary to "get tough" with a witness. On such occasions, it is important that the lawyer's tough demeanor be warranted under the circumstances. The lawyer's "get tough" attitude must be seen by the judge or jury as warranted given the witness's behavior. In other words, just as in international diplomacy, a measured and proportional response is preferred.

The Adverse Witness

An adverse witness is an opposing party witness or a witness identified with the opposing party. Witnesses identified with the opposing party include employees, relatives (frequently true in child welfare cases), business partners, and witnesses who share a community of interest with the opposing party. Because an adverse witness is expected to be somewhat uncooperative with opposing counsel, leading questions can be used to control the witness, even if the lawyer is calling the witness on direct examination.[3]

It is common practice to alert the court and counsel that one is calling an adverse witness, although it should be obvious when the witness is the opposing party. The court has the discretion to interpret whether a witness is adequately aligned or identified with the opposing party to warrant being labeled an adverse witness. Formal protocol includes asking the witness several foundational questions that establish adversity, followed by a request that the court designate the witness as adverse and allow leading questions.

Using adverse witnesses is not the norm. Call adverse witnesses sparingly and with caution, because such witnesses are likely to promote their interests and not yours. It also allows opposing counsel to cross-examine his or her own witness using leading questions.

However, there may be occasions when calling an adverse witness is necessary to prove an element of your case or defense. Agency counsel may wish to call a parent to prove paternity or an element of dependency. Parent counsel may wish to call a caseworker to show hostility toward his client.

The Hostile Witness

A hostile witness is an adverse witness who does not become adverse until demonstrating hostility while testifying. The lawyer may ask the judge to declare a witness hostile based on that hostility or unwillingness to answer. As with the adverse witness, counsel may use leading questions on direct examination.[4]

Impeachment

Impeachment is the term used to describe the process of discrediting a witness's testimony. Although trial lawyers typically focus on impeachment by prior inconsistent statement, any presentation of evidence that tends to discredit a witness is a form of impeachment. The most commonly recognized and used forms of impeachment are impeachment by prior inconsistent statement and impeachment by omission.

---

3. FED. R. EVID. 611(c).
4. *Id.*

A well-conducted impeachment on a significant matter can bolster one's case significantly. Conversely, a sloppy or confusing impeachment, particularly on an insignificant matter, can make the lawyer (and by association the client) appear petty and disingenuous. One should impeach, therefore, only on significant matters.

Similarly, impeachment where an inconsistency or omission is reasonable and easily explained can backfire. One should impeach, therefore, only where the inconsistency or omission is clearly a violation of veracity that cannot be repaired by re-examination by the other side. Remember, the rule of completeness[5] allows opposing counsel to request a complete reading of the impeachment source where the impeachment is taken without full context.

Counsel may impeach on direct or cross.[6] It is generally not advisable to impeach one's own witness, particularly where the witness has simply forgotten the information, in which case, the technique of refreshing recollection can be used.

Finally, do not impeach merely because you can. Impeachable testimony may not damage one's case and may, in fact, enhance it.

> *Impeachment will be as persuasive as the prior*
> *statement is credible.*

Impeachment by Prior Inconsistent Statement

The most commonly used—and arguably the most useful—form of impeachment is impeachment by use of a prior statement that is inconsistent with the current statement. It is presumed that the prior statement made by the witness is more trustworthy than the current statement, and therefore, that the witness is not telling the truth while testifying. This is particularly true when the prior statement is a statement made under oath that was not corrected or contradicted until now. While one may impeach with various types of previous statements, including a mere unrecorded comment, an impeachment will be as persuasive as the prior statement is likely to be credible. Previous sworn testimony is, therefore, the best source of impeachment.

Impeachment is best accomplished by use of the Three Cs Technique:

---

5. FED. R. EVID. 106.
6. FED. R. EVID. 607.

> **The Three Cs Impeachment Technique**
>
> **Confirm**
> Confirm that the witness did just now make a statement that you know to be inconsistent with a prior statement.
>
> **Credit**
> Credit or bolster the existence and veracity of the prior statement.
>
> **Confront**
> Confront the witness with the prior inconsistent statement.

> Q: Ms. Worker, Mr. Father is a responsible father, correct?
>
> A: No, I don't believe so.

At this point, the witness has made a statement that the lawyer knows to be inconsistent with a prior statement.

Confirm:

> Q: It is your testimony that Mr. Father is not a responsible father?
>
> A: That's correct.

Credit:

> Q: You testified in a hearing in this matter three months ago on January 15, 201_.
>
> A: Yes.
>
> Q: You were under oath at that time?
>
> A: Yes.

Confront:

> Counsel: I'm showing a copy of Ms. Worker's testimony from the January 15, 201_, hearing in this matter to counsel. May I approach the witness?
>
> *Showing opposing counsel.*
>
> I'm showing you a copy of your testimony from the January 15, 201_, hearing. Please look at page 2, line 6, and

> read along with me silently to yourself as I read aloud:
> *Question:* Was this dad a responsible father? *Answer:* Yes.

Q: Ms. Worker, that's what it says, correct?

or

Q: I read that correctly?

A: Yes.

You should lead the witness through the Three Cs with clear, short, direct, and firm declarative statements. It is also wise to retain control of the situation by reading the prior inconsistent statement yourself and not allowing the witness to do so. Note that the impeachment is complete once the witness acknowledges that the previous statement is as read by counsel. Do not make the mistake of going beyond this point and venturing into a discussion that might lead to an explanation for the inconsistency. And never ask: "So were you lying then or are you lying now?"

Note: Documents used for impeachment are not offered or entered into evidence. Do not conflate the process for impeachment with the process for introduction of an exhibit. Some courts may still want counsel to mark the impeachment document for identification purposes only.

Impeachment by Omission

Impeachment by omission is similar to impeachment by prior inconsistent statement; howerever, rather than referencing a prior inconsistency, one references the nonexistence of information in a prior source in which the opportunity for the information existed. The key to omission impeachment is the assumption that if the current testimony were accurate, such information would have been provided before in the prior source. Impeach by omission only if it is obvious that if the information were true, it would have been mentioned before.

Q: Ms. Worker, Mr. Father has never physically abused the children's mother, correct?

A: Yes, he did abuse her.

At this point, the witness has made a statement that the lawyer knows is important, but was not included in a prior statement where such information would have been highly relevant.

Confirm:

Q: It is your testimony that the Mr. Father physically abused the mother?

A: That's correct.

Credit:

Q: You completed a report to the court dated January 15, 201_.

A: Yes.

Q: You were truthful in that report?

A: Yes.

Q: And it is your complete report?

A: Yes.

Q: You prepared this report in order to give the court an accurate picture of family dynamics?

A: Yes.

Q: And it is important that you include all relevant matters that could affect the outcome of the case?

A: Yes.

Q: Physical abuse of a mother by a father is an important factor?

A: Yes.

Confront:

Q: Ms. Worker, no where in your report do you mention that Mr. Father physically abused the mother.

At this point, the witness or opposing counsel may ask to see a copy of the report. In such cases, you should provide it and allow the witness to review it. This should not be viewed as a problem, but rather a mistake for the opponent, who will look silly if not incredible as she pretends to try to find the omission in the report.

Refreshing Recollection

A witness is required to testify from memory. That is why a witness may not generally refer to a document while testifying. An exception is the use of a document[7] to refresh a witness's memory. If a witness cannot recall something the witness once knew, the lawyer is permitted to refresh the witness's memory by using a document, photograph, or other object. The process requires that the witness indicate

---

7. FED R. EVID. 612.

that the witness cannot remember something, that a certain document or object would help the witness recall, and that having looked at the document or object the witness can now recall. The document or object is then removed from the witness, and the witness may answer the question from a refreshed memory. The document used to refresh is not placed in evidence, but some courts may want it marked for identification purposes.

Q: Mr. Worker, when did you first speak to the foster mother?

A: I don't remember the date.

Q: Is there anything that would help you remember?

A: Yes, my incident report.

Q: I am showing a copy of the incident report to counsel.

Q: May I approach the witness?

Q: I'm handing you a copy of your incident report. Please review it silently and let me know when you are finished.

The witness indicates he is finished.

Q: I'll take your incident report back from you now. Now do you remember?

A: Yes.

Q: When did you first speak to the foster mother?

A: July 15, 201_.

Recorded Recollection[8]

Although much less common in practice than refreshing recollection, recorded recollection or past recollection recorded is a useful tool. The rule of recorded recollection permits a witness to read from a document, which would then fall under a hearsay exception.

Think of recorded recollection as the next step in an unsuccessful refreshing of recollection. Where a witness is unable to recall a matter of his or her own memory, even though the matter can be found in the document, for example, the witness may read the answer if proper steps are followed.

The hearsay exception of recorded recollection requires that a witness testify that the witness cannot testify accurately about a matter once known without using the

---

8. FED. R. EVID. 803(5).

document. The record must have been made or adopted by the witness when the information was fresh and could have been recorded accurately. The document is not placed in evidence unless offered by the adverse party.

Having previously attempted to refresh recollection:

Q: It is your testimony that you do not have a recollection of the date you first visited the foster mother even after reviewing your incident report?

A: Yes.

Q: You did at one time know the date, correct?

A: Yes.

Q: And you prepared the report with the date in it?

A: Yes.

Q: And you did that when the information was fresh in your mind?

A: Yes.

Q: And the information was accurate when you recorded it?

A: Yes.

Counsel: I am going to give the incident report back to you now.

Q: Please read the sentence that describes when you first visited the foster mother.

A: "I went to the foster family home on July 15, 201_, and this was the first time I met Mrs. Foster, the child's foster mother.

Special Witnesses

Some witnesses present management issues simply by virtue of their status as infirm, very old, or very young, for example. Courts may permit leading questions on direct examination in such cases under Fed. R. Evid. 611(c), which allows leading "as may be necessary in order to develop the witness' testimony." The Advisory Committee Note to the rule against leading on direct includes exceptions for "the witness who is hostile, unwilling, or biased; the child witness or the adult with communication problems . . . ." Under such circumstances, counsel should ask the court's permission to lead as necessary, citing this rule and comment.

The Child Witness

Much is written in the legal and psychological literature about the child witness. The child witness presents a unique challenge for the child welfare attorney in terms of preparation, competence, and manner of examination. It is a subject far too voluminous and complex to cover in detail in this publication.[9] The child witness is, however, specifically named as an exception to the rule against leading, and counsel is justified in asking for permission to lead, especially with a very young child witness.

At the same time, the child welfare attorney calling the witness on direct should be mindful of the impact leading questions may have on the fact finder. Because children are believed to be highly susceptible to suggestion, the fact finder may devalue testimony derived through leading questions.

Preparation is key to successful child witness examination; it also helps the child. Lawyers should take advantage of child development experts to help make the child comfortable and able to communicate in a developmentally appropriate manner. When this is done, testimony can be successful without causing undue harm to the child.

Recall that all witnesses, including children, are presumed competent to testify under the federal rule.[10] The presumption is in effect until challenged by counsel; when that happens, a competency hearing may be held by the court. Children are typically deemed competent if it can be demonstrated that the child has personal knowledge of the matter,[11] the ability to remember and communicate, awareness of veracity, and the meaning of an oath.[12]

---

9. *See* ANNE GRAFFAM WALKER, HANDBOOK ON QUESTIONING CHILDREN, A LINGUISTIC PERSPECTIVE, 2d Ed. (American Bar Association 1999); SHERRIE BOURG CARTER, CHILDREN IN THE COURTROOM: CHALLENGES FOR LAWYERS AND JUDGES, 2d Ed. (NITA 2009); JOHN E.B. MYERS, EVIDENCE IN CHILD ABUSE AND NEGLECT CASES (Wiley Law Publications 1997).

10. FED. R. EVID. 601.

11. FED. R. EVID. 602.

12. FED. R. EVID. 603; *See also* JOHN E.B. MYERS, LEGAL ISSUES IN CHILD ABUSE AND NEGLECT PRACTICE, 2d Ed. (Sage 1998).

CHAPTER SEVEN

EXHIBITS AND THEIR FOUNDATIONS "PICTURE THIS!"

If it doesn't fit, you must acquit.[1]

> ### *Take-Away*
> *Eight Steps:*
> *Mark, Show, Approach, Identify, Lay Foundation (HARPO*[2]*),*
> *Offer, Publish, Use*

If a picture paints a thousand words, lawyers are well advised to use fewer words and more pictures. While most evidence is testimonial, evidence is also received through the introduction and use of exhibits. As such, fact finders can not only be *told* what happened by the witnesses, they can be *shown* what happened with exhibits. In this way, fact finders can experience the evidence rather than struggle to construct it through the witness's recounting. In other words, the fact finder can use his or her own sensory perceptions to see, feel, hear, or otherwise *experience* the evidence. As child welfare lawyers seek to tell the complex story of the family, exhibits, including photographs, drawings, letters, reports, toys, and weapons can prove highly useful.

Categories of Exhibits and Their Use

Commentators typically divide exhibit evidence into three categories:

1. Real evidence exhibits

2. Demonstrative evidence exhibits, and

3. Documentary (writings) evidence exhibits

---

1. Defense counsel's statement to the jury in closing argument in *People v. Simpson*, SC 031947 (1996), regarding "People's Exhibit 77," the blood stained gloves allegedly worn by "the murderer." The defendant, O.J. Simpson, struggled to put them on. The exhibit and demonstration led to defense counsel's successful and famous closing argument theme using the gloves as a metaphor for inadequate evidence.
2. Hearsay, Authentic, Relevant, Personal Knowledge, Original.

These distinctions among the categories of exhibit evidence are useful for organization, introduction, and use. The distinctions will, however, be vague at times and some evidence may fit more than one category.

Some commentators include a fourth category of exhibit evidence—called "illustrative evidence exhibits"—for those exhibits that illustrate testimony (such as a diagram), but are not fair and accurate representations, so they cannot be admitted as demonstrative exhibit evidence. In this chapter, such exhibits are referred to as "purely illustrative exhibits," and not evidence, because they are typically not offered or admitted in evidence.

Additionally, lawyers may occasionally use "visuals," which are lawyer-generated aids and not evidence; examples include the "writing out" of points made by the witness on a white board or the electronic projection of the elements of termination in closing argument.

Real Evidence Exhibits

Real evidence is tangible evidence that played an actual part in the issues at trial, as opposed to being lawyer-generated for the purposes of trial. A traditional example of real evidence in a criminal trial is the gun used to murder the victim. In child welfare cases, real evidence includes such things as clothing, a child's toy, or instrumentalities used to harm a child, such as a belt. Audio and video recordings are typically regarded as real evidence. Photographs can be categorized as demonstrative or real.

Real evidence can be used to persuade the fact finder that a particular version of events is true by making the event seem more real and by showing that the explanation is logical. Where a child was whipped with the buckle end of a belt, seeing and touching the actual belt provides visceral persuasion. At the same time, the configuration of the belt buckle can be shown to be consistent with the injury marks on the child.

Demonstrative Evidence Exhibits

Demonstrative evidence is typically lawyer-generated and used to illustrate testimony. Demonstrative exhibits are not part of the "res gestae" of the case and, therefore, cannot be categorized as real evidence. Demonstrative exhibits simply help the witness tell the story. Demonstrative exhibits in a child welfare case include charts, diagrams, medical models, drawings, dolls, and sometimes photographs.

A social worker may use a diagram of a family home as a demonstrative exhibit to help describe the proximity of and access to the various rooms. A physician may use a chart of water temperature and corresponding burn rates to help describe the length of time it would take to cause an immersion burn under various scenarios.

Note: Similarly, a purely illustrative exhibit may be used to illustrate testimony without satisfying the demonstrative exhibit foundation of authenticity (fair and accurate depiction). Such an exhibit is not typically offered into evidence. For example, a physician might be allowed to illustrate the whiplash effect of shaking a baby by shaking a doll even though the doll is not a fair and accurate example of a child's physical makeup.

Documentary (Writings) Evidence Exhibits

Documentary evidence refers specifically to writings. In child welfare cases, documentary evidence typically includes reports, letters, business records, and public records. Documentary evidence purports to document a past occurrence with someone's recorded writing. As such, documentary evidence can be persuasive proof.

Hearsay is an issue with all documentary evidence.

Child welfare cases are typically replete with written reports by caseworkers and mental health professionals. Jurisdictions frequently rely on such reports, especially from caseworkers, to prove abuse, neglect, and best interests of the child. Child welfare lawyers should not only use such documentary evidence, but should also be prepared to object to their use where adequate foundation does not exist.

Foundation

All testimony requires some foundation.[3] Before a neighbor may testify that she saw a parent hit a child, for example, it must be established how the witness recognizes the parent and child. The same is true for exhibit evidence. The witness through whom the exhibit is introduced must be able to establish that he has sufficient *familiarity* with the exhibit—that the witness knows what it is.

Next, the witness must establish that the exhibit is authentic based on the witness's knowledge.[4] *Authenticity* refers to the requirement that the evidence is what it purports to be. A witness must simply testify, for example, that the belt is the belt that was retrieved at the abuse scene.[5]

---

3. FED. R. EVID. 104.
4. More than one witness may be used to lay foundation if necessary. In such instances, evidence may be offered conditionally. FED. R. EVID. 104(b).
5. *See* FED. R. EVID. 901(a).

As with all evidence, admissibility of exhibit evidence depends on its ***relevance***. Relevant evidence is evidence that tends to make a fact at issue more or less probable.[6]

Beyond witness familiarity (basic foundation), authenticity, and relevance, additional evidentiary foundation may be required depending on the type of evidence offered. For years, NITA trainers have used the acronym HARPO[7] as a checklist of all the elements of evidentiary exhibit foundation. These elements are explained in the following chart and illustrated by specific evidence type later in this chapter.

Exhibit Foundation Elements
HARPO

Hearsay Fed. R. Evid. 801

Does the exhibit contain an out-of-court statement offered for the truth of the matter asserted for which there is no non-hearsay or hearsay exception provision?

Authenticity Fed. R. Evid 901

Is the exhibit what it purports to be?

Relevance Fed. R. Evid. 401

Does the exhibit tend to make a fact at issue more or less likely?

Personal Knowledge Fed. R. Evid. 602

Can the witness authenticate the exhibit from personal knowledge?

Original Fed. R. Evid. 1001

Is the requirement of an original writing or substitute satisfied?

---

6. FED. R. EVID. 401, 402.

7. HARPO: Hearsay, Authenticity, Relevance, Personal Knowledge, Original. Additional Ps can be added to include unfair prejudice and privilege. Some trainers reverse the order to create the acronym OPRAH.

Pretrial Admission of Exhibits

The admissibility of evidentiary exhibits can be established prior to trial by court order brought about by motion or stipulation. The Federal Rules of Civil Procedure provide for a pretrial conference process wherein the court may rule on the admissibility of proposed evidence.[8] State court rules of civil procedure typically include a similar process, and dependency courts may use such processes or rely on their own dependency court rules. Once the admissibility of exhibits is settled, you can create an original trial exhibits notebook and copy notebooks to prepare for and be used at trial. The efficiency of such processes benefits the litigants, counsel, and the court.

Introducing Exhibits at Trial

The nature of dependency court is such that most exhibits are introduced "on the fly" at trial. Even so, it is good practice to organize all exhibits prior to trial and provide counsel with copies.

Exhibits are introduced through a long-standing protocol grounded in trial practice convention, common law, and codified rules of evidence and civil procedure. The process varies somewhat by jurisdiction and local practice. Leading questions are allowed because they are foundational by definition. You should know the full and formal process described below and make modifications as your local practice dictates.

Step 1: Preliminary Foundation

The introduction process for all exhibits begins with the following "preliminary foundation."

1. **Introduce the topic that will lead to the introduction of the exhibit.**

   > Q: Ms. Worker, did you see the condition of the mother's apartment?
   >
   > A: Yes.

2. **Mark the exhibit.**

   > *Mark the exhibit with exhibit stickers used by your court.*

---

8. FED. R. CIV. P. 16(c)(2)(c).

3. Show the exhibit to opposing counsel.

   I am showing a copy of what has been marked for identification as Petitioner's Exhibit A to opposing counsel.

4. Request permission to approach the witness.

   Your Honor, may I approach the witness?

5. Hand the proposed exhibit to the witness and indicate the same.

   I am handing you what has been marked for identification as Petitioner's Exhibit A.

6. Ask the witness if she recognizes the exhibit.

   Q: Do you recognize this?

   A: Yes.

7. Ask the witness what the exhibit is.

   Q: What is it?

   A: It is a photograph of the kitchen in the Respondent Mother's apartment.

Once the witness has identified the proposed exhibit, the preliminary foundation is complete. The witness may not yet testify about the contents of the exhibit because it is not yet in evidence. Note that prior to admission of an exhibit, it is referred to as that which "has been marked for identification as Exhibit A."

Step 2: Substantive Foundation

Having identified the exhibit through the preliminary foundation process, you should proceed to the substantive foundation required for the particular type of evidentiary exhibit. This will vary from two or three questions for a diagram or photograph to a detailed list for a business record. Below, we continue with the example of a photograph.

1. Establish how the witness recognizes the photograph.

   Q: How do you know this is a picture of the mother's kitchen?

   A: I visited the apartment and went into the kitchen.

2. **Establish the time.**

> Q: When were you there?
>
> A: August 1, 201_.

3. **Establish fairness and accuracy at that time.**

> Q: Is this photograph a fair and accurate depiction of the kitchen on August 1, 201_?
>
> A: Yes

Optional; required for Illustrative Exhibits.

> Q: Would the exhibit help you explain your testimony?
>
> A: Yes.

The substantive foundation is now complete. The **relevance** should be obvious because it concerns the condition of a home in a dependency case. The most basic foundation of **personal knowledge** has been established by the witness's statement that she visited the apartment and saw the kitchen. The **authenticity** of the photograph has been established by the witness's statement that the photo is a fair and accurate depiction of the kitchen on the date specified. Note that it is not necessary to establish who took the photograph.

The R, P, and A of HARPO are satisfied. The H and O, hearsay and original writing, are not components of a demonstrative exhibit such as a photograph.

Step 3: Offer the Exhibit

> Your Honor, I offer Petitioner's Exhibit A.

Step 4: Objections

Immediately following the offer, opposing counsel may object or voir dire the witness. Judges typically ask whether there is any objection at this point. Counsel should make and meet objections using the protocol described in chapter eight. Assuming that there is no objection or the objection is overruled, the court will admit the exhibit. At this point, the name of the exhibit changes from that which "has been marked for identification as Exhibit A" to simply "Exhibit A."

Step 5: Publication

Following admission, counsel should immediately publish the exhibit to the court and jury by inquiring as follows: "Your Honor, may I publish Exhibit A."

The word *publication* is the term of art used in the rules. It simply means "show," which is the word preferred for juries and by some judges. Publication can include handing a photograph to the judge or jury, distributing copies to the jury, or electronically projecting the image by overhead/Elmo projector or computer projection. "Blow-ups" are also allowed, although they are being replaced by electronic projection in many courts.

Step 6: Use the Exhibit

Do not stop with publication. Merely introducing an exhibit is of limited value and can confuse the fact finder. Use the exhibit to persuade the jury of the point for which the exhibit is introduced. Ideally, the exhibit becomes *part of* the witness's testimony—the witness's oral testimony can now be demonstrated and illustrated by the exhibit.

Q: What was the condition of the house?

A: Filthy.

Q: Using Exhibit A, please describe why you say the house was filthy.

A: OK. First of all, there was rotting food left out. If you look at the picture, you can see old rotting food pieces on the kitchen table in the middle of the photo.

Q: Are there other examples of why you say the house was filthy?

A: Yes, again in this photo, this time at the top of the photo by the sink, you can see piles of dozens of dirty dishes and even a dirty diaper by the sink.

Selected Child Welfare Exhibit Foundations

Applying the concepts of foundation, relevance, and authenticity will guide you well when introducing exhibits. Applying all of the elements of HARPO will fill in the gaps. Still, do not depend on this analysis and your ability to memorize foundations. It is far better to compile a written list of common foundations and make it a part of your trial notebook. The following is a list of selected child welfare court exhibits and their substantive foundations. "Preliminary foundation" is assumed.

Real Evidence

Weapon or Other Tangible Object (unique; no chain of custody required)

1. Determine that the witness recognizes the object.

2. Determine that the witness recognizes the object because of a unique characteristic.

3. Determine that the object is in the same or substantially similar condition as at the relevant time.

> Q: Officer, how is it that you recognize this knife?
>
> A: It is the knife I found at the father's house.
>
> Q: How do you know it is the same knife?
>
> A: Because I examined it carefully and recognize it. Also, it is unique in that it has the initials JB carved on the blade.
>
> Q: Is it in the same or substantially similar condition as when you found it at the father's house?
>
> A: Yes.

Weapon or Other Tangible Object (not unique; chain of custody required)

1. Determine that the witness recognizes the object.

2. Determine that the witness or someone else protected the condition through an unbroken chain of custody.

3. Determine that the object is in the same or substantially similar condition as at the relevant time.

> Q: Officer, how is it that you recognize this knife?
>
> A: It is the knife I found at the father's house.
>
> Q: How do you know it is the same knife?
>
> A: Because I recognize it and because it is in the evidence bag that I placed it in at the father's house.
>
> Q: What did you do with it after you placed it in the bag?
>
> A: I logged it into evidence storage that evening.
>
> Q: When did you next see it?
>
> A: Today when I checked it out of evidence storage to bring here.

Q: Has it been in your possession since you logged it out?

A: Yes.

Q: Is it in the same or substantially similar condition as you found it at the father's house?

A: Yes.

Demonstrative Evidence

Photograph, Diagram, or Chart[9]

1. Determine that the witness is familiar with the scene pictured.

2. Determine that the scene pictured is a fair and accurate depiction of the actual scene at the time in question.

3. Determine that the exhibit will assist the testimony for good measure (technically only required for illustrative evidence).

Q: How do you recognize this as a diagram of the apartment waiting area?

A: I live in the apartment building, and so I go through the waiting area every day.

Q: Is this diagram a fair and accurate representation of the apartment waiting area on August 1, 201_.

A: Yes.

Q: Will it assist you in giving your testimony? (*optional*)

A: Yes.

Tangible Object / Model Used for Demonstration

1. The witness identifies the model in preliminary foundation.

2. Establish that it is a scale model.

3. Establish that as a scale model, it is a fair and accurate representation of the type of object at issue.

---

9. Where a photograph, diagram, or chart (or even a physical model) is not prepared to scale, such as where the lay witness has drawn a diagram, the witness may testify that it is not to scale but is the best the witness could do and that it would aid the testimony. It can then be used for illustration without introduction. Some courts may accept it in evidence based on indicia of reliability.

4. Establish that it would assist the witness in giving testimony.

Q: Doctor, is this a scale model of a child's brain?

A: Yes.

Q: As such, is it a fair and accurate model of a child's brain?

A: Yes.

Q: Would it assist you in explaining the injury the child received?

A: Yes.

Medical Imaging (x-ray, CT scan, PET scan, and MRI)[10]

1. Establish that the witness recognizes the image as that of the patient.

2. Establish that it is a fair and accurate image.

3. Establish that it would be helpful in explaining the testimony.

Q: Doctor, how do you recognize this as the x-ray of the patient's left arm?

A: I examined the patient, ordered the x-ray, and reviewed the x-ray.

Q: Is this x-ray a fair and accurate representation of the patient's left arm at the time you examined the arm?

A: Yes.

Q: Would it assist you in explaining the nature of the patient's injury?

A: Yes.

Audio[11] and Video Recording

1. Establish that the operator recorded the event.

2. Establish that the operator was familiar with the recording equipment.

3. Establish that the equipment was in good working order.

4. Establish that the witness observed the event.

---

10. Some courts may view medical imaging as real evidence.

11. More detailed foundations may be necessary for certain recordings, such as one for which a claim of illegal recording has been made.

5. Establish that the recording accurately and fairly captured the event.

6. Establish that the recording has been protected (chain of custody).

7. Establish that the recording is unchanged and still accurately captures the event.

> Q: Mr. Worker, you said that you recognize this as a video and audio recording of your interview with the child. Who recorded it?
>
> A: I did.
>
> Q: Are you trained to use the recording equipment?
>
> A: Yes, it is part of my regular duties.
>
> Q: Was the equipment working properly?
>
> A: Yes.
>
> Q: Did you observe the event?
>
> A: Yes, I was there and participated in it.
>
> Q: Did the recording accurately and fairly depict the event?
>
> A: Yes, I watched it that day, and it was fair and accurate.
>
> Q: Where has the recording been kept?
>
> A: Logged in and locked in our video storage closet.
>
> Q: Is it still fair and accurate?
>
> A: Yes.

The foregoing foundation establishes the authenticity of the recording. The recording, however, is still potentially hearsay if it is offered for the truth of the matter asserted. In such cases, a nonhearsay justification (admission by a party opponent for example), or a hearsay exception (child hearsay rule) must be found.

Introduction of a 911 emergency child abuse recording raises admission issues. First, you must authenticate the recording by voice recognition of the speaker or through an "assigned number" type presumption.[12] Next, again, a hearsay solution must be found.

---

12. FED. R. EVID. 901(b)(6).

Documentary (Writings) Evidence Exhibits

Documentary evidence brings in the previously discussed foundation elements of HARPO (authenticity, relevance, and personal knowledge) plus special consideration for the elements of hearsay and original writing. All documents are potentially hearsay and may not be entered in evidence without a showing of nonhearsay or a hearsay exception.[13] Documents may be nonhearsay because they are not offered for the truth of the matter asserted or because they are admissions by a party opponent.[14] Typical hearsay exceptions include the business records and public records exceptions. Take note that documents frequently contain hearsay within hearsay — a statement in the document refers to yet another statement. All hearsay must be accounted for in order for the document to be admitted. Alternately, nonconforming parts of the document may be redacted.

Next, the requirement of the original writing rule, formerly and less accurately known as the best evidence rule, must be satisfied. The rule, which has nothing to do with whether a document is the best evidence for a proposition, is concerned with whether the document being offered is sufficiently authentic.[15] Historically, that required an original, but that is no longer the case. Rather, the current federal rule provides that a duplicate (copy) of the original satisfies the rule unless a genuine issue has been raised as to the authenticity of the original itself (a claim, for example, that the original is a forgery).[16]

Business Record (Fed. R. Evid. 803(6))

Business records are documents made and kept in the regular course of business, such as reports, logs, medical records, and memoranda. The business records exception is an exception to the hearsay rule. Again, there may be inadmissible hearsay within hearsay.

A document from a child protection service agency (CPS) can be a business record, although some jurisdictions may consider them public records.[17] A document

---

13. FED. R. EVID. 801.

14. FED. R. EVID. 801(c), 801(d)(2).

15. FED. R. EVID. 1002.

16. FED. R. EVID. 1003. Part (2) also prohibits a copy for "unfairness" although this is rarely a concern.

17. *See* FED. R. EVID. 803(8), (9). The foundation for a public record is similar to a business record and concern records kept by a public agency as required by law and regarding the agency's work. A public record is also a hearsay exception. Public records include records of activities kept by government agencies, usually as required to do so by law or regu-

prepared by CPS specifically for court, such as a caseworker report to the court will probably not be considered either a business or public record, but may be admitted under special court rules that specifically address the admission of such reports. Even in such cases, however, be alert to nonadmissible components of the report, such as hearsay within hearsay.

1. Establish that that the record was made at or near the time of the event that it records.

2. Establish that the record was made by a person with such knowledge (formerly referred to as a business relationship) or based on information from such a person.

3. Establish that the record is *kept* in the course of regularly conducted business activity.

4. Establish that the record was *made* as part of the regular practice of that business activity.

> Q: When was this memo written?
>
> A: On the day of the interview with the caseworker.
>
> Q: Who wrote the memo?
>
> A: I did.
>
> Q: How were you familiar with the information that you were recording?
>
> A: I was the person who had the conversation with the caseworker.
>
> Q: Do you normally keep such memos in the regular course of your business?
>
> A: Yes, we are required to keep records of our worker conduct reviews.
>
> Q: Do you write or make such memos in the regular course of your business?
>
> A: Yes, we are required to write memos of our worker conduct reviews.

---

lation. Police reports are not public records for purposes of criminal prosecution, but are, arguably, in a dependency case.

Private Writings / Letters / Written Correspondence (Fed. R. Evid. 901(b)(2))

Letters or other types of traditional correspondence must be authenticated, typically by a lay witness who recognizes the handwriting or signature. An expert witness in handwriting analysis may also authenticate such documents. Additionally, the reply letter doctrine can be used to authenticate a letter's author by testimony that one sent a letter and a letter was received in reply.[18]

Remember that this step satisfies the matter of authenticity, not hearsay.

The following is an example of a lay witness authentication of a letter received from a sender whose handwriting is recognized.

1. Establish that the witness recognizes the handwriting.

2. Establish that the witness is familiar with the handwriting.

3. Establish how the familiarity is sufficient.

> Q: How do you know that this is a letter from Mr. Hancock?
>
> A: I recognize the handwriting.
>
> Q: Anything else?
>
> A: I recognize the signature (either handwriting or signature is sufficient).
>
> Q: How are you familiar with the handwriting and signature?
>
> A: I have known Mr. Hancock for years and have seen his handwriting and signature many times.

Electronic Documents (fax, e-mail, Web site contents)

Electronic communications are a standard means of communication in both personal lives and in business. In a sense, it is almost naïve to categorize them separately from other writings. They are, in fact, simply written communications that are transmitted differently—electronically rather than by mail. The elements of HARPO still apply to these types of exhibits. As to the authenticity element, look to the rules for private writings and business records.

Such documents can be authenticated by process or circumstantially. Whereas process authentication for a mailed document or reply letter doctrine includes testimony of placing a properly addressed and postage paid envelope in a mailbox, a

---

18. FED. R. EVID. 901(b)(9).

fax or e-mail version will simply involve testimony that the witness placed the document in the fax machine and pushed the send button or clicked the e-mail send button. The circumstantial authentication method will involve testimony that the document contains the sender's fax number, e-mail address, or has the company logo on it. The process for identifying a signature will be identical to that used for nonelectronic documents. At this point, remember that authentication is but one element of HARPO and that the documents must also pass the hearsay test.

Web and social networking sites also contain written material and may be offered as documentary evidence. Such sites can be considered virtual file cabinets where documents are kept. Authentication, therefore, requires identifying the site name and address to show that it is what it purports to be: a printout of a posting from a specific site.

Facebook (FB) Post

1. Establish how the witness recognizes the post.

2. Establish how the post was printed.

3. Establish that it is a true and accurate depiction at the specific time.

Q: How do you recognize this as a post from Mr. Father's FB page?

A: I visited, that is I went to his FB page, and I saw and read this very post.

Q: How did you do that?

A: I am a "FB Friend" of Mr. Father, and so I can go to his page and read his "wall posts." And that is what I did.

The foregoing constitutes process authentication.

Q: How else do you recognize this?

A: I can see by just looking at it that it is a posting from Mr. Father's site?

Q: How do you know that?

A: I've been to his FB page and this is identical.

Q: Anything else?

A: Yes, it has his "profile picture" and name on it at the top.

The foregoing constitutes circumstantial authentication.

Q: What did you do after you read this post?

A: I printed it from my computer to my printer.

Q: Is this that printing?

A: Yes.

Q: Is this a fair and accurate depiction of what was posted on the FB page on the date you viewed it?

A: Yes, it's identical.

CHAPTER EIGHT

MAKING AND MEETING OBJECTIONS
ENFORCING THE RULES OF THE TRIAL

Objection, your Honor, what's that got to do with anything! [1]

> **Take-Away**
>
> *Enforce and abide by the rules of trial.*
>
> *Object to form and substance to support case story.*
>
> *Make short, clear, recognized, and professional objections.*
>
> *Make and meet objections with precision and professionalism.*
>
> *Focus on the Big Three: Relevance, Foundation, and Hearsay.*

Objections are the trial conduct equivalent of the Rule of Law in societal conduct. Absent such rules, justice is elusive. The objections process is the means by which we control the integrity and reliability of information and thereby enhance the probability of just outcomes.

Justice for children and their families is the goal of the child welfare court process. It is, therefore, imperative that the rules of the trial be enforced in child welfare court. Child welfare counsel should not accept a culture of relaxed enforcement of the rules of process and evidence so often present in child welfare courts. To the contrary, if we are dedicated to justice, we should be dedicated to rules that enhance just outcomes. [2]

Child welfare lawyers have a duty to learn and use the objection process for the benefit of their clients. This requires an understanding of the rules of evidence, the form of objections, and the protocol for making and meeting objections.

---

1. This was an objection made by an enthusiastic but forgetful mock trial student during competition. The objection was sustained on the ground of relevance.
2. "Relaxed" advocacy as a court culture is inappropriate. The author recognizes, however, that many jurisdictions loosen or relax evidentiary standards by law in dependency court, particularly in the disposition phase, for purposes of "judicial economy." Regardless of the wisdom of such policy, attorneys are required by law and ethics to follow the law of their jurisdictions.

Two Categories of Objections[3] [4]

Form

An objection to form is one that maintains that the question as formed will elicit evidence improperly, even though the substance of the evidence may be admissible. Examples include leading, compound, and argumentative questions. Objections to form promote reliable evidence by requiring that witnesses testify from their memory based on understandable questions. Form objections may also be made to answers that are beyond the scope of the question, such as narrative or non-responsive objections. Objections to form of the question must be timely and thus be made before the witness answers.[5]

Substance

An objection to substance is one that maintains that the information sought is inadmissible under the law. Examples include relevance, foundation, and hearsay. Objections to substance promote reliable evidence by requiring that the information sought satisfies the scrutiny of the law of evidence. Substantive objections must also be timely—they must be made as soon as the objectionable nature of the material sought becomes apparent.[6] Substantive objections may be made to a question or an answer. Where the witness has provided objectionable material on the record, the objection must be combined with a motion to strike in order to remove the inadmissible evidence from consideration.

The Purpose of Objecting

The decision to object should be based on the theory and theme of the case. With substantive evidentiary objections, you should object if excluding the evidence serves your story of the family. Do not object simply because there is a ground for the objection. It is possible that objectionable material may promote your case. With form of the question objections, you should object to ensure predictable and responsive testimony.

Objections should be made to:

---

3. A comprehensive pocket-sized objections reference for trial is BRIGHT, CARLSON, IMWINKELRIED, OBJECTIONS AT TRIAL, 5th Ed. (NITA 2008).

4. *See generally* FED. R. EVID. 611 for the courts authority to manage objections. The rule gives the court authority to control witness examination to ensure the ascertainment of truth, avoid delay, and protect witnesses.

5. FED. R. EVID. 103.

6. FED. R. EVID. 103.

Exclude Evidence Prejudicial to One's Case

Object to all evidence that may prejudice your case. Be sure there is a recognized basis for the objection.

Protect a Witness from Improper Questioning

Object if your witness is being improperly questioned or treated. Examples include argumentative questions and questions that assume facts not in evidence.

Preserve an Issue for Appeal

Fed. R. Evid. 103 provides that failure to object at trial waives the right to appellate consideration. The exception is the rule of "plain error," which has limited application on which you should not be rely. Rule 103 also provides that objections must state the specific ground for the objection unless it is obvious. Do not rely on a belief that the ground for objecting is obvious.

Objections should only be made where there is a good-faith basis for the objection. While you should be mindful of the reaction that objecting has on the judge or jury and use objections wisely, excluding prejudicial evidence is the paramount concern.

The Objection Process Protocol

Making the Objection

- Stand up completely.

- State the objection to the judge, not to counsel.

- State the objection forcefully but professionally.

- State the objection concisely, citing the basis (no rambling "speaking" objections), for example:

  - Objection! Hearsay

  - Objection! Relevance

  - Objection! Leading

- Remain standing until the judge rules on the objection.

- If the judge allows opposing counsel to argue, listen carefully and respectfully to the argument.

- If the judge allows further argument, make it. If you believe you have a significant point to be made, ask the judge if you may be heard.

- Receive the court's ruling with professionalism and sit down. No comment is necessary. Do not thank the judge for the ruling.

- You have the right to voir dire the witness to determine the evidentiary foundation for the information sought.

Meeting the Objection

- When the objection is made, stop and listen to it.

- Remain standing.

- Ask the judge for the opportunity to be heard. Respond tactfully, but quickly before a ruling. Do not assume the court wants argument and just begin speaking.

- Argue to the court, not opposing counsel, when explaining why the objection is not valid.

- With the exceptions of rephrasing leading, compound, or vague questions, do not abandon your question just because there is an objection.

- If it is clear that you failed to lay adequate foundation, you may simply advise the court that you will lay further foundation and then do so.

- Receive the court's ruling with professionalism and sit down. No comment is necessary. Do not thank the judge for the ruling.

- If the objection is sustained, consider making a conditional offer or offer of proof if necessary.

Conditional Offer[7]

To the extent that the admissibility of testimony you are eliciting is tied to later testimony, you may offer the evidence conditioned on the introduction of subsequent testimony. Following the objection, ask the court for permission to make a conditional offer and either promise to "tie it up" later or state (outside the presence of the jury) the nature of the evidence that will be introduced later. This situation typically arises regarding foundation or relevance. If you are opposing a conditional offer, remember to move to strike the evidence at the close of the opposition's case if the condition is not met.

---

7. FED. R. EVID. 104

Offer of Proof [8]

It may be necessary to make an offer of proof regarding crucial evidence when such evidence is excluded by objection. In order for an appellate court to rule on whether the exclusion was reversible error, there must be a record of the excluded evidence. Ask the court for an opportunity to make an offer of proof and either have the witness testify or make a statement of what the evidence would have been. This must be done outside the jury's presence. The offer may also educate the court into reconsidering its prior ruling.

Witness Voir Dire

A lawyer may engage in limited voir dire of an opposing witness to determine the admissibility of evidence being offered. The lawyer may object and ask for an opportunity to voir dire or simply ask to voir dire. Following the voir dire, state the grounds for the objection or indicate that there is no objection. Witness voir dire typically occurs when opposing counsel tenders a witness as an expert or offers an exhibit as evidence. While witness voir dire is directed to the issue of admissibility, it may have the effect of diminishing the weight of the evidence as well.

Eight Essential Objections as to Form

1. *Leading* (Fed. R. Evid. 611)

The question suggests the answer and is objectionable on direct. Leading questions are allowed on cross-examination, to lay foundation, and for special witnesses such as the old, young, or infirm.

Agency Counsel:	Ms. Worker, the Agency has three previous incidents of contact with the Jones family, correct.
Parent or Child Counsel:	Objection, leading!
Agency Counsel:	It is foundational, your Honor.
Ruling:	Sustained. Whether and to what extent the agency has prior contact is a substantive matter to which the witness must be required to testify from her memory, not the lawyer's prompting.

---

8. FED. R. EVID. 103.

2. Compound

The question is two separate questions not necessarily susceptible to one answer. Questions asked to establish a relationship between two facts are not objectionable.

Child's Counsel (Cross):	Ms. Jones, you felt the temperature of the water before you put the baby in the tub, correct?
Agency Counsel:	Objection! Compound question.
Child's Counsel:	It is not a compound question, your Honor, because it seeks to establish the relationship and sequence between the actions of testing the temperature and putting the baby in the tub.
Ruling:	Overruled.

3. Vague

The question is likely to get an ambiguous answer because it is confusing or incomplete.

Agency Counsel:	Officer, what happened on August 23?
Parent Counsel:	Objection! Vague.
Response:	I'll rephrase, your Honor. Officer, what did you first see when you arrived at the hospital on August 23?

4. Argumentative

The question pressures the witness to accept questioner's conclusion or interpretation rather than a fact. Sometimes thought of as "badgering the witness."

Parent Counsel:	Mr. Worker, your hatred for this mother causes poor decision-making, doesn't it.
Agency Counsel:	Objection! Argumentative.
Ruling:	Sustained.

5. Narrative

Applies to questions and answers. A lawyer may not ask for information that requires a narrative answer, and a witness may not give a narrative answer. Witnesses are required to answer specific questions so that opposing counsel can defend against improper information through objections. It is difficult or impossible to predict what is coming next in a narrative. Long but responsive answers are not narrative.

Child's Counsel:	Mr. Jones, please tell us about your family.
Agency Counsel:	Objection! The question calls for a narrative.
Child's Counsel:	Your Honor, the question is specific as to data about the family.
Ruling:	Sustained. Counsel, you may ask the witness for specific *types* of data about the family.

6. Asked and Answered

A question may not be repeated to the same witness. The lawyer may ask a variation or clarification of a previous question.

Agency Counsel:	What did Ms. Jones tell you about who caused the child's injury?
Answer:	She said she hit her with an open hand because the child was out of control.
Agency Counsel:	Excuse me, who hit the child?
Parent Counsel:	Objection! Asked and answered.
Ruling:	Overruled. The clarification is appropriate because the answer was not definitively stated. You may answer the question.
Answer:	The mother said that she *herself* hit the child.

7. Assuming Facts Not in Evidence

It is objectionable to use an unproven fact as a predicate or condition to a question. This typically arises on cross-examination.

Parent Counsel:	Doctor, you were in such a hurry to get to your next patient that you only examined the child for three minutes.
Agency or Child Counsel:	Objection! Assumes facts not in evidence. It has not been established that the doctor was in a hurry.
Ruling:	Sustained.

8. *Nonresponsive*

You may move to strike an answer that does not respond to the question or to that part of the answer that exceeds the responsive part. In most jurisdictions, both the lawyer asking the question and opposing counsel may object to nonresponsive answers.

Child Counsel:	Why didn't you take the baby to the hospital right away?
Answer:	Because I didn't know she was hurt badly. Otherwise I would have. This story they have concocted about how I waited until I thought I would get into more trouble isn't true. I have always taken my kids to the doctor if they were hurt. When my oldest son broke his arm . . . .
Agency Counsel:	Objection! Nonresponsive! Move to strike everything after "Otherwise I would have . . . ."
Child's Counsel:	Your Honor, the additional information is responsive because it explains why she did not take the baby to the hospital in the context of the agency's version. This mother should be allowed to tell her version.
Ruling:	Sustained. She can tell her version in response to specific questions. The information offered by the witness after the words "Otherwise I would have" is stricken.

Substantive Objections[9]

Motion in Limine

Some evidence may be so potentially prejudicial that even a sustained objection at trial is insufficient protection from its harmful effect. The motion in limine is the tool to exclude such evidence before trial. The motion is generally not granted unless the evidence is not only subject to a sustainable objection at trial, but is so damaging that once mentioned, its impact cannot be managed by a sustained objection. Motions in limine are traditionally reserved for jury trials[10] and, therefore,

---

9. The "rulings" illustrated in this section are based on the author's analysis of the federal rule without respect to specific jurisdictional law.
10. FED. R. EVID. 103(c).

are less common in child welfare court. They may be used, however, even in bench trials as a way to manage a complex and highly significant evidentiary matter before trial. Because child welfare court is institutionalized and involves many of the same litigants and judges over and over, the motion in limine may also have the effect of settling evidentiary disputes for future proceedings as well. If granted, the evidence is excluded and the offering party may not attempt to introduce it at trial. If the motion is denied, you may still object at trial.

An example may be an agency's attempt to introduce evidence of a mother's post-filing conduct in the adjudication phase. Because the petition may presumably be granted only on a showing of its justification at the time of filing, such evidence should be excluded as any discussion of it leaves an unfairly prejudicial impact, even on the court. Respondent Parent attorneys may also prefer such evidence be excluded as a practice.

Eleven Essential Trial Objections as to Substance

1. *Relevance* (Fed. R. Evid. 401, 402)

The information sought does not make a fact at issue more or less likely. The following uses the same evidentiary issue discussed in Motion in Limine above.

Agency Counsel:	Mr. Worker, what did the father tell you he would do if ordered to go to anger management classes?
Parent or Child Counsel:	Objection! Relevance.
Agency Counsel:	Your Honor, it is relevant because it tends to prove the parents unwillingness to learn better parenting.
Parent or Child Counsel:	May I be heard on this point, your Honor? It may or may not prove such willingness, but that is not the issue at this adjudication proceeding. The only issue is whether the petition alleging abuse can be sustained based on the allegations of such abuse prior to the filing. Counsel's argument goes to disposition and is not relevant here.
Ruling:	Sustained.

2. *Foundation*[11]

Foundation for a particular piece of evidence, testimonial or physical, is the predicate information required as a condition to allowing the testimony. Foundation is the indicia of reliability that makes the evidence admissible. In its most basic form, for example, the foundation for a witness to testify that a light was green is the predicate testimony by the witness that the witness was present and saw the light. While this example would best be handled under lack of personal knowledge, it is the essence of foundation. Foundation objections more typically relate to admissibility of exhibits such as business or public records, or the foundation for lay and expert opinions.

Parent Counsel:	Doctor, as this mother's therapist, what is your opinion about the welfare of the children while in her care?
Child or Agency Counsel:	Objection! Lack of foundation.
Ruling:	Sustained. The doctor is qualified as an expert witness in adult behavioral psychology, not as a placement expert. Further, the doctor has not evaluated the children and, therefore, has no foundation to offer an expert opinion on the children's welfare.

3. *Lack of Personal Knowledge* (Fed. R. Evid. 602)

Witnesses must testify, generally, from their sensory perceptions, about what they observed or did. In other words, they must know what they are talking about.

Parent or Child Counsel:	Ms. Neighbors, would you say that Ms. Jones is an attentive mother?
Agency Counsel:	Objection! Lack of personal knowledge.

---

11. Foundation is its own specific objection. But lack of personal knowledge, improper lay opinion, and speculation are also foundation-type objections, and there is, in practice, some overlap and conflation of these four objections that is often overlooked by the court. An objection as foundation that might better be categorized as lack of personal knowledge may well be sustained.

Parent or Child Counsel:	May I be heard, your Honor? As the next-door neighbor, this witness has observed Ms. Jones's parenting for two years, giving her the requisite foundation, i.e., personal knowledge through observation, to testify to attentiveness.
Ruling:	Overruled as to lack of personal knowledge.

4. *Improper Lay Opinion* (Fed. R. Evid. 701)

Lay or fact witnesses cannot offer opinions unless those opinions are rationally based on the witness's perception.

Agency Counsel (to a worker *not* qualified as an expert witness):

Q: Mr. Worker, what is your observation of the mother's emotional condition?

A: I believe she is very fragile and unpredictable due to what appears to be an underlying mood disorder.

Parent or Child Counsel:	Objection! Improper lay opinion. Move to strike.
Agency Counsel:	May I respond, your Honor? This caseworker has observed this mother for over a year before making this assessment, which is, therefore, rationally based on the witness's perception.
Ruling:	Overruled in part: The witness may testify to fragile and unpredictable as they are rationally based perceptions. Objection sustained as to underlying mood disorder, which is an expert opinion in mental health. That portion is stricken from the record.

5. *Speculation*

The witness may not speculate, particularly about someone's feelings, state of mind, or motivation.

Parent or Child Counsel:	Mr. Father, why didn't your wife take the baby to the hospital right away?
Agency Counsel:	Objection! Speculation.
Ruling:	Sustained.

6. Unfair Prejudice

The probative value of the information is outweighed by the danger that it will cause unfair prejudice.

Agency Counsel:	Doctor, using exhibit 1, the doll, please demonstrate the physical reaction of a child's head when the body is shaken violently.
Parent or Child Counsel:	Objection! Unfair prejudice. The doctor has already described the reaction, and any evidentiary value this demonstration may have is outweighed by the prejudicial impact this demonstration on a doll might have.
Ruling:	Overruled. The demonstration is likely to show the physics of the head movement, adding to the doctor's testimony, which, in turn, is highly probative of the central abuse allegation in this case.

7. Confidentiality and Privilege (Fed. R. Evid. 501)

Statute and common law provide for certain privileges, including attorney-client, psychotherapist-patient, physician-patient, and marital. Privilege, contrasted with confidentiality, is a right by the holder of the privilege not to be forced to testify on a matter. The privilege holder can waive the privilege and certain jurisdictional exceptions exist.

Confidentiality is the ethical rule that prevents a disclosure of another's confidence, typically outside of a court setting.

Agency Counsel:	Your husband told you he "had had it with these children," correct?

Parent Counsel: Objection! My client wishes to invoke her right under the marital privilege and decline to answer this question.[12]

Ruling: Madam, you may choose to not answer the question.

* * *

Parent Counsel: Doctor, please tell us what the child said to you about his sister.

Child Counsel: Objection! Confidentiality and privilege. My child-client's communications with his therapist are protected by the psychotherapist-patient privileged and have not been waived by him or his guardian ad litem. This witness is, therefore, precluded from disclosing such information because of its confidentiality.

Ruling: Sustained.

8. Settlement Offers (Fed. R. Evid. 408)

Settlement offers and offers made during settlement negotiations are not generally admissible.

Agency Counsel: Ms. Worker, was this mother at any time prior to today agreeable to supervised visitation?

Parent or Child Counsel: Objection! Inadmissible settlement offers testimony. Any discussions regarding this matter were held as part of mandatory mediation.

Ruling: Sustained.

9. Judicial Notice (Fed. R. Evid. 201)

A court may take judicial notice of facts generally known, not open to dispute, or capable of ready ascertainment, including certain judicial adjudications.

---

12. *See* Trammel v. United States, 445 U.S. 40 (1980).

Agency Counsel:	(*to parent*) It is only three blocks from the court-house to social services, correct?
Parent Counsel:	Objection! Asks for speculation.
Agency Counsel:	Your Honor, I ask the court to take judicial notice of the fact that it is three city blocks form this courthouse to social services.
Parent Counsel:	Objection! Improper judicial notice.
Ruling:	Overruled. This fact is generally known to be true and is capable of ready ascertainment. To require additional proof would be a waste of judicial time. The court takes judicial notice of the fact that it is three city blocks from this courthouse to social services.

10. *Improper Character Evidence* (Fed. R. Evid. 404)

Character evidence cannot be used to prove a person acted in conformity with such character. Character evidence may be used:

- 404(b): to show motive, opportunity, intent, preparation, plan, knowledge, identity, or absence of mistake or accident

- 608(a)(b): to attack reputation as to truthfulness or rebut the same

- 608(b): to show untruthfulness

- 609: to show criminal convictions for a felony or a crime of dishonesty, which occurred within ten years (except for juvenile adjudications).

Agency Counsel:	Mr. Jones, you were convicted of writing several bad checks to Nita Discount Liquor last year, correct?
Parent Counsel:	Objection! Improper character evidence. Any such matters were not felony convictions.
Ruling:	Overruled. True, they are not felonies, but bad check convictions constitute offenses involving dishonesty under Rule 609.

11. *Hearsay* (Fed. R. Evid. 801(c))

Hearsay is "a statement other than one made by the declarant while testifying at trial or hearing, offered in evidence to prove the truth of the matter asserted." Certain prior statements that appear to be hearsay may be admitted as nonhearsay and still others may be admitted as exceptions to hearsay. Documents can be hearsay or hearsay in part. Evidence can contain hearsay within hearsay. A witness's own prior statements can be hearsay.

- Not Hearsay (801(c)): Not offered for the truth of the matter asserted.

- Not Hearsay (801(d)): The witness's own statement and fits certain additional criteria.

- Not Hearsay (801(d)(2): An admission by a party opponent.

- Hearsay exceptions include:

  - Present Sense Impression (803(1))

  - Excited Utterance (802(2))

  - State of Mind (803(3))

  - Statements Made for Medical Diagnosis (803(4))

  - Business Records (803(6))

  - Statement Against Interest 804(b)(3)

  - Residual "Catch-All" Exception 803(24)

  - Child Hearsay Exception[13]

  - Dependency Court Disposition Phase and Other Local Exceptions

Parent Counsel:

Q: What did Ms. Worker say to you about getting your kids back?

A: She said she would see to it I never get my kids back.

Agency Counsel: Objection! Hearsay. Move to strike.

---

13. Typically requires the child be under ten and if not present, there must be corroborating evidence. Many jurisdictions also require a pretrial hearing. *See* John E.B. Myers, Evidence in Child Abuse and Neglect Cases, 3d Ed, §7.53 (Wiley Law Publications 1997).

| Parent Counsel: | May I respond, your Honor? It is not hearsay because it is offered as an admission by a party opponent under Rule 801(d)(2). |
| Ruling: | Overruled. |

Trial lawyers can feel intimidated by evidentiary objections. Remember that most evidentiary issues arise in three areas: relevance, foundation, and hearsay. Facility with these "Big Three" will serve you well.

The "Big Three" Evidentiary Objections

Relevance: Makes a fact at issue more or less likely

Foundation: The witness possesses this knowledge base (includes foundation, speculation, lay witness opinion, and lack of personal knowledge)

Hearsay: It is not hearsay because it is not offered for the truth, is an admission by a party opponent, or satisfies one of the exceptions

---

Opening Statement and Closing Argument Objections

Objections during opening statement and closing argument are allowed, but should be used cautiously. Likewise, judges are disinclined to sustain objections during openings and closings unless there has been a clear and even egregious violation. Remember than turnabout is fair play. Nonetheless, counsel has an obligation to object where objectionable statements can harm one's case. The following are the most common objections during openings and closings.

Opening Statement

1. Improper Argument

    a. Arguing the Facts

    b. Arguing the Law

    c. Arguing the Credibility of a Witness

2. Referencing Inadmissible Evidence

3. Addressing the Jurors by Name

4. Expressing a Personal Opinion

Closing Argument

1. Stating or arguing facts not in evidence

2. Misstating facts

3. Misstating the law

4. Expressing a personal opinion

5. Arguing the golden rule

6. Appealing to the jurors prejudice

7. Exceeding the scope of rebuttal

Avoid Drawing Objections

Good questions get good answers, and good questions avoid objections. Check your work for objectionable material:

1. Avoid leading questions on direct examination by using the "six honest words": *who, what, where, when, why,* and *how.*

2. Ask for facts, not conclusions or opinions (except for expert witnesses and rare lay witness opinions).

3. Be sure the witness has a foundation for the answer.

4. Be sure the information sought is relevant to your case.

5. Do not ask for hearsay without knowing the exception or nonhearsay rule.

CHAPTER NINE

OPENING STATEMENT
IMPRINTING THE STORY

This is a case about a mother's love . . .

her love for alcohol and cocaine.[1]

Take-Away

Imprint the case story through a persuasive evidence preview.

Identify issues, explain contentions, address opposition, and ask for relief.

Do not argue.

Opening statement is the process of imprinting the story of the case in the fact finder's mind at the outset of the trial. It is the first thing the fact finder will hear about the case. Given that people are most likely to accept that which they hear first (principle of primacy), it is a critically important opportunity. Persuade the fact finder of your position at opening statement.

The importance of imprinting a case story at the outset of the trial holds true for bench as well as jury trials. Judges are human. They become interested . . . and they become bored. They can become confused, but when they have clarity and interest they become invested. Given that many dependency court judges hear these cases daily, it is all the more important that we successfully imprint a case story so that the judge does not see the current case as just another child abuse case.

At its foundation, the opening statement is a *preview of the evidence* to come. In the opening statement, we tell the fact finders what they will hear. In direct and cross-examination, they hear what has been previewed. In closing argument, we argue the meaning of the evidence they have heard. For all of this to come together successfully, we must begin with a persuasive preview. And an evidentiary preview becomes persuasive when it is told in the context of the story of the case, the story of the family.

---

1. From a petitioner's opening statement in a Los Angeles County Dependency Court bench hearing.

In an organizational sense, opening statement is an abstract of the entire trial so that the fact finder has a *context* in which they hear the evidence. As is often said, opening statement is a kind of road map, user's guide, or program for the trial, although such analogies are not recommended as story-telling devices. With such analogies in mind, however, you can give the trial a context through a compelling presentation of the case story.

Without the context of the case story, a fact finder may fail to take notice of important evidence or place undue import on other evidence as it is revealed. Remember, each witness does not tell the whole story of the case, and so it is important that the fact finder understand which portion of the story a particular witness is telling and how it fits into the whole.

The end goal of opening statement is to leave the fact finder understanding and believing your story of the family.

Preparation

Preparing the opening typically occurs last in the sequence of case preparation tasks. Once you have prepared all of the evidence and drafted the closing argument, you are in an ideal position to determine precisely what you should say to begin the trial. Because it is imperative that you engage the fact finder at the outset of the trial, do not read an opening nor rely heavily on notes. Nor should you memorize the opening. Many successful trial lawyers prepare a detailed script and then reduce the script to key bullet points for occasional reference as necessary.

Opening Statement Principles

Imprint the Story of the Case

Use the brief time allotted for opening statement to tell your story of the family. It is imperative that the fact finder hears and understands your story of the case from the outset so that it is imprinted in the fact finder's mind from the beginning of the trial. Your story should begin with a *persuasive grabber* or phrase that encapsulates the story. This could be a story device. From there, communicate the case theory and theme.

Although your story is formulated by the testimony of the witnesses, do not tell the story witness by witness, even though that makes preparation easier. Rather, tell the story in a logical sequence and *weave in the witnesses' testimony*.

> *Tell the story in a logical sequence and weave in the witnesses' testimony.*

Consider telling the story in the *present tense* for persuasive effect. Rather than saying, "The child tiptoed down the hall and peeked into her father's room," say instead, "The child tiptoes down the hall and peeks into her father's room."

Promises

Make *promises that you can keep*. It is important to tell the fact finder what the testimony will show. It is a serious error to promise something you may not be able to deliver or to overstate or exaggerate your proof.

Bad Facts

Deal with the *bad facts*. They are part of your story. It is better that you bring up and explain bad facts that you know the other side will present rather than allow the fact finder to discover them from the other side. This does not mean that you restate the opposition's case. It does mean that you face head on those things that will be presented as clearly inconsistent with your case theme.

Brevity

Opening statement in a child welfare matter should be brief, perhaps no more than five or ten minutes. Where the court culture discourages opening statements, ask the judge to allow for a brief opening to provide a structure for the evidence. Use only two to three minutes and build your credibility with the judge. Once the court comes to appreciate the value of your opening statement to the trial process, expand but do not abuse the opportunity.

Jurors want and need opening statements. It would be unfair to require a juror to listen to the evidence without an organizational structure and preview. Judges, conversely, tend to be impatient with opening statements, especially in bench trials. Still, judges can benefit from an organizational structure and evidence preview, so you should not waive or fail to request opening statement, even in bench trials.

Do Not Argue Facts

Argument is not allowed in opening statement; it is reserved for closing argument. No evidence has been presented at the time of opening statement so there is no opportunity for you to argue. It is objectionable to do so.[2]

---

2. Objections during closing argument are also covered in the chapter on objections.

Lawyers have difficulty defining exactly what crosses the line from statement into argument. As a general rule, if a witness will make the statement that you wish to make, it is not argument. This is why, although it is not required, lawyers frequently preface their evidentiary statements in opening with phrases like *the evidence will show*, or *this witness will testify that* . . . . When in doubt about whether something is argument, test the statement by placing those *predicate phrases* before the statement.

The prohibition against argument does not require that the fact statement be uncontroverted. To the contrary, you must tell your client's side of the story.

Professor Steven Lubet suggests two additional tests to determine whether information is argument. The *verification test* suggests that a nonargumentative fact can be verified, whereas an argumentative conclusion cannot. Additionally, the *link test* suggests that information becomes argument when it requires a rhetorical link in the verification chain.[3] A simple common-sense test that combines all three tests above might be to simply ask: "Is this *my statement*, or is it found in the record?"

Do Not Discuss the Law

It is impermissible to discuss the law in opening statement. Again, that is reserved for closing argument, where the law can be discussed and argued. It would seem, therefore, that any mention of the law is objectionable;[4] however, such is not the case. Court convention has developed in most jurisdictions that allows a brief statement of the law of the case to provide context for the factual statements.

For example, in a dependency case a lawyer may tell the jury that the case is about child abuse, that the state contends this child was abused, and that the judge will advise them later that child abuse is intentionally causing serious physical harm to a child. However, you could not begin to discuss how and why one's evidence proves that. The legal statement can be tested in part by the qualifier *the judge will instruct you later that* . . . .

Crossing the line into legal discussion in a bench trial is less of a concern. Still, you should avoid it, except to give brief context to the facts.

Do Not Give a Civics Lecture or Use Filler

Many an opportunity to capture the fact finder and imprint the story of the case has been squandered with civics lectures and other filler that do not persuade the

---

3. STEVEN LUBET, MODERN TRIAL ADVOCACY: ANALYSIS AND PRACTICE, 4th Ed., 375 (NITA 2009).
4. Objections during opening statement are also covered in the objections chapter.

jury. There is very little value in explaining to the jurors that we all have a role to play in the American system of justice. Likewise using time to thank jurors for coming today does little to promote your case; worse, it can be seen as disingenuous—the jurors are well aware that they had no choice in the matter. Such discussions are typically no more than a lawyer's crutch.

Engage the Fact Finder

The key to persuasion is engagement. We must *connect* with the fact finder. Engaging with the fact finder requires us to be physically and emotionally accessible.

Do not read a script or notes. Talk to the fact finder. *Eye contact* is essential.

Open up to the fact finder. Do not keep a physical barrier between you and the fact finder (unless the court rules require you to do so). At the same time, do not invade the fact finder's personal space. Stay a reasonable distance. Test this with colleagues—ask them when they feel you are too close for comfort. The goal is to stand and deliver. Face the jury, plant your feet, and begin. Then move with purpose. Change positions when you change ideas or parts of the story. Do not be a statue or a nervous pacer.[5]

Do not fake sincerity. Demonstrate appropriate levels of genuine emotion. Neither histrionic nor monotone deliveries are persuasive. Your emotion should match the case and the fact being described. Use strong voice volume and inflection. Emphasize the power words in your sentences.

Use Exhibits and Visuals

There is no prohibition against using a potential exhibit in opening statement, yet lawyers are frequently apprehensive to do so. You should use powerful visuals in opening statement to help tell your story. Do not use exhibits that you intend to introduce at trial unless you are reasonably certain they will be admitted. If those exhibits are not admitted, this is something opposing counsel will most certainly point out in closing as an evidentiary promise you did not keep and which must not be considered. Use AV projection to enhance the exhibit where appropriate.

You may also use purely illustrative aids, which will not be introduced as evidence. You may wish, for example, to simply write the key evidence you will present in bullet points on a flip chart and point to them as you work through your statement.

---

5. NITA Instructor and Denver trial court judge Robert McGahey explains this form of engagement in the words of the famous actor James Cagney who explained successful acting as follows: "learn your lines, plant your feet, look the other actor in the eye, say your lines, and mean them."

Suggested Opening Statement Organization

Introduction

Capture the fact finder with a one- to two-sentence "grabber" that articulates your case theme. Follow with a short abstract of the case story. Introduce yourself and your client in a jury case where this may not be already known.

> *This case is about a mother's love . . . her love for alcohol and cocaine. And it is about the terrible consequences to a small child as a result of the mother's addiction. From the date of her birth two years ago, a child named Tina has been neglected by her mother. This mother's neglect has included failing to feed her baby (sometimes for more than a day), clothe her baby, wash her baby, and pick up her baby after hours of her screaming in her crib. It has included failing to care for her baby when her baby was sick or take the baby to the doctor when she had a high fever. This two-year-old little girl has lived a life deprived of the basic necessities of life.*

> *My name is Mark Baker, and I represent the State of Nita Department of Family Services. Seated at the table over here with me is Jim Caldwell, the caseworker from Family Services who is working to care for baby now.*

The Issues

Indicate the issue or issues the fact finder will be asked to decide. Include an introduction to the standard of proof. Feel free to define the party's contentions. Mention the law of the case briefly and only to give context to the facts and issues.

> *You are here to decide whether the child Tina Thomas is a neglected child under the laws of our state. We will prove to you that this little girl is indeed a neglected child. The proof will come from witnesses who will tell you what they saw, what they heard, and what they did. This proof will constitute something called proof by a preponderance of the evidence. You don't need to worry now about exactly what that means, and Judge Steinhauser will explain all that to you at the end of the trial. For now, just know that it means something is more likely than not to have happened.*

> *Now, Tina's mother, Mrs. Jo Watson, contends that her baby is not neglected and that the State of Nita, through Caseworker Caldwell, should not have removed her from the home. We disagree. And so we will put on evidence that will show you that the baby had to be removed for her own safety.*

The Evidence / The Story

Tell the story of the case in detail—comprised of the legal theory and theme—using story devices. Tell the story in the present tense, as though it were happening right at that moment. Mention what a particular witness will say when it adds persuasion or clarity.

> *The baby girl Tina Thomas was born on July 15, 201_, at Nita General Hospital. The next day, Tina went home with her mother. From that point forward, Tina's life would be filled with neglect, pain, fear, and loneliness.*

> *It is 6:00 p.m. on the evening of July 16, 201__. Tina Thomas is one day old. Tina is alone in her crib, in a urine-soaked diaper, hungry. She cries and cries, but no one comes. No one is home . . . .*

The Other Side

Cases that do not settle typically have legitimate factual disputes. Briefly address the opposition's key evidence that the fact finder must reconcile to accept your theory of the case.

> *It is no easy matter to be a single mother living in poverty. Mrs. Watson did indeed need to be looking for a job, as she will tell you she was doing. But the evidence will show that what she was out looking for was not a job, but her drug dealer.*

The Relief

Be absolutely clear about the relief you are seeking. The judge and jury should not be the least bit confused about what they are being asked to decide.

> *The Nita Department of Family Services asks you to declare that the baby girl Tina Watson is a neglected child under the laws of Nita, and that as a result, the Department is entitled and obligated to take temporary custody of her, care for her, and provide services to her and her mother.*

CHAPTER TEN

ETHICS AND PROFESSIONALISM
INTEGRITY IN THE COURTROOM

> **Take-Away**
>
> *Lawyers are officers of the legal system,*
> *citizens with special responsibilities for the quality of justice,*
> *and representatives of clients.*
>
> *Trial lawyers are all of these things in the courtroom.*

Lawyers are officers of the legal system, citizens with special responsibilities for the quality of justice, and representatives of clients.[1] As trial lawyers, we are all of those things when we step into the courtroom. Our responsibility must be to conduct ourselves with integrity at all times when it comes to these duties. Our integrity is demonstrated by the qualities of honesty and consistency of professional character.

We must adhere to our professional codes of conduct. Each state has adopted a version of the ABA Model Code of Professional Responsibility or the ABA Model Rules of Professional Conduct.[2] These codes define the lawyer's duties of independent, competent, and zealous advocacy.[3] They also provide detailed guidance on myriad issues that arise in the courtroom.

Lawyers representing agencies, parents, and children in child welfare cases are, like all lawyers, bound and governed by these codes. Because we work in a unique and specialized forum, we sometimes forget this. We should not. Children and families are entitled to rely on their lawyers, too.

Yet we see, for example, lawyers talk to children outside of the presence and consent of the child's attorney. We see agency counsel discussing active cases with judges outside of a hearing or the presence of opposing counsel. Perhaps worst of all, we see lawyers representing children fail to meet basic advocacy requirements, such as seeing the child client or meaningfully participating in hearings. These practices are disallowed by our ethics codes for good reason and we must, as a profession, adhere to these professional standards.

---

1. THOMAS D. MORGAN & RONALD D. ROTUNDA, 2004 SELECTED STANDARDS OF PROFESSIONAL RESPONSIBILITY 3.

2. A majority of states have adopted a version of the Model Rules of Professional Conduct.

3. MODEL RULES OF PROF'L CONDUCT, Preamble, Model Rule 1.1.

It is appropriate to acknowledge the uniqueness of the child welfare court system. It is a specialized and institutionalized forum with unique procedures. It is also a relatively young forum. Child welfare courts, as currently comprised, did not become formalized until the 1970s. In response to the need for clarification on certain unique issues of the evolving child welfare court system, several specialized ethics codes have been developed. While none of these codes has been adopted in its entirety by the various jurisdictions, portions of these codes have been adopted. Additionally, these codes serve as important persuasive authority on difficult ethical issues that may not be covered in our general ethics codes. Lawyers working in child welfare court should be familiar with these in addition to their state ethics codes. There are:

- ABA Standards of Practice for Lawyers Who Represent Children in Abuse and Neglect Cases (1996)[4]

- ABA Standards of Practice for Lawyers Representing Child Welfare Agencies (2004)[5]

- ABA Standards of Practice for Attorneys Representing Parents in Abuse and Neglect Cases (2006)[6]

Additionally, lawyers must be familiar with any state case law, statute, or local rule defining the unique ethical duties of the child welfare attorney.[7]

Selected Child Welfare Courtroom Ethics Issues

The following are intended to provide guidance for some commonly occurring child welfare court ethics issues. [8]

Competence

Competence is perhaps the most basic ethical duty of the lawyer. A lawyer may not take a matter to court that the lawyer is not competent to handle. Competence includes knowledge, skill, thoroughness, and preparation.[9] Child welfare cases are complex and time consuming. Lawyers should never be afraid to admit they are

---

4. www.abanet.org/child/repstandwhole.pdf.

5. www.abanet.org/child/agency-standards.pdf.

6. www.abanet.org/child/clp/ParentStds.pdf.

7. *See, e.g.,* In re J.E.B., 854 P.2d 1327 (1993) (children's counsel); COLO. REV. STAT. § 19-1-111; SUPREME COURT DIRECTIVE 04-06 (2004).

8. For a comprehensive discussion of child welfare court ethics, *see* JENNIFER L. RENNE, LEGAL ETHICS IN CHILD WELFARE CASES (American Bar Association 2004).

9. MODEL RULES OF PROF'L CONDUCT, R. 1.1.

overwhelmed and need help. Additionally, no lawyer can perform competent representation without adequate time and resources. Child welfare lawyers must be careful not to exceed reasonable caseloads.[10]

Loyalty

The duty of loyalty provides that the lawyer abide by the client's directives regarding the objectives of representation.[11] While the client does not dictate trial strategy, the client does dictate the goals of the litigation, including whether to admit to or deny the accusations and how they wish the case to be disposed.

Agency lawyers must, at the outset, know to whom to be loyal—that is, who the client is. In an "agency model" the client is the agency itself, as represented by the caseworker or supervisor (the agent of the agency). In such cases, the lawyer may not substitute her judgment for that of the client. In the "prosecutorial model" where a city, county, district, or state attorney brings the action, the state, and not the department is considered to be the client. Here, the prosecutor is bound to serve "the people" and may, therefore, choose not to follow the agency's directive.[12]

This is an even more difficult issue for children's counsel and varies significantly depending on the model of advocacy. In a "pure attorney" model, which exists in a minority of jurisdictions, the traditional rules of client direction apply. In an "attorney / guardian ad litem" model, existing in the majority of jurisdictions, the lawyer is typically charged with representing the child client's best interests, and is, therefore, allowed to substitute her judgment for the client's. Even here, however, lawyers must be careful not to substitute judgment just because their view differs from that of the child client. Some authority suggests that a predicate to the substitution of judgment must be that the client's wishes are not just unwise but seriously harmful.[13] In any event, lawyers representing children should always consider the child's perspective[14] and not become overly paternalistic.

---

10. *See* Kenny A. v. Perdue, 532 F.3d 1209, 1214 (11th Cir. 2006), where the court held that unreasonably high caseloads for child's counsel prohibited competent representation and deprived children of effective assistance of counsel.

11. MODEL RULES OF PROF'L CONDUCT, R. 1.2.

12. ABA STANDARDS OF PRACTICE FOR LAWYERS REPRESENTING CHILD WELFARE AGENCIES (2004).

13. ABA STANDARDS OF PRACTICE FOR LAWYERS WHO REPRESENT CHILDREN IN ABUSE AND NEGLECT CASES (1996).

14. "Representing Children and Youth" in CHILD WELFARE LAW AND PRACTICE, MARVIN VENTRELL & DONALD DUQUETTE 511 (Bradford 2005).

A duty of loyalty ethical issue is less likely to occur when representing parents. Still, lawyers should be careful to honor their client's autonomy and not act in a paternalistic fashion.

Diminished Capacity

Diminished capacity is an omnipresent ethics issue in child welfare court. By definition, a child client is a minor, and therefore, presumably has varying levels of capacity relative to various litigation issues. Diminished capacity is also an issue for many parent clients as a result of drug addiction, mental illness, or low cognition.

Model Rule 1.14, as amended in 2002, provides the general rule that there is a presumption of full capacity and that when dealing with a client with diminished capacity (presumably where the lawyer questions the client's capacity to make an important decision), the lawyer shall, as far as possible, maintain a normal attorney-client relationship. This means that even where some evidence of diminished capacity exists, the lawyer shall work to adhere to loyalty, confidentiality, diligence, competence, communication, and advice.[15] Comment 1 to Model Rule 1.14 provides, regarding the child client, that children as young as five are regarded as having opinions entitled to weight regarding their custody.

There will, however, be occasions where a client's capacity is so sufficiently diminished that the client cannot guide the attorney regarding an objective of representation. The first order of business in this instance is to assess capacity objectively and not simply assign lack of capacity, particularly just because the lawyer disagrees with the client. Comment 6 to Model Rule 1.14 provides a list of assessment factors for the child client including the ability to articulate consequences and consistency of views.

It is also important to view capacity as existing on a continuum and with degrees. In other words, a client should not be deemed incapacitated once and for all as to all matters. To the contrary, clients may have varying degrees of capacity on varying subjects. This recognition was a major justification for the 2002 amendment to Model Rule 1.14 that changed the rule from "Representing a Client with a Disability" to the current rule, "Representing a Client with Diminished Capacity."

As a last resort, where a client's directive is absent or erroneous due to diminished capacity, the lawyer may take protective action. These actions include making the decision for the client after consulting with family and professionals, requesting a

---

15. RENNE, *supra* note 8.

reconsideration period to clarify or improve circumstances, requesting the appointment of a guardian for the client, and withdrawing.[16]

Communicating with Parties

Model Rule 4.2 prohibits counsel from communicating with represented parties without the other lawyer's consent or the judge's special order. This can be tricky in child welfare court because counsel and the agency caseworker have so much interaction with each other and the parties. This is particularly true of the child's attorney and the caseworker. Still the rule must be followed. Reasonable contact can occur without counsel present or other authority as long as the contact does not involve "the subject of representation." Counsel for a child or parent should, for example, be able to speak with the caseworker to arrange meetings with their clients without specific permission from agency counsel.

Trial Publicity

Most child welfare proceedings in most jurisdictions are closed and confidential. There is ongoing debate in the policymaking community of the wisdom of open versus closed proceedings, and there is evidence of a trend toward more open proceedings. Lawyers must follow the law of their jurisdictions.

Model Rule 3.6(a) prohibits lawyers from making out-of-court statements that they know will be disseminated by the media and that have a substantial likelihood of materially prejudicing the adjudicative proceeding. Commentator Renne, under the exceptions of part (b), reasons that agency lawyers may discuss information in the public record and may state that an investigation is in progress. Renne also says that a parent lawyer may make statements that protect a client from substantial undue prejudicial effect of recent publicity not initiated by the lawyer.[17] Additionally, courts may issue gag orders on all parties prohibiting statements to the media.

Cross-Examination Ethics

A full and fair cross-examination is essential to the production of justice. Still, it is not an "anything goes" proposition. Although bias and credibility are always permissible areas of inquiry, it is unethical to ask a question that does not have a good-faith basis in fact. Even though the witness may deny the baseless fact, unfair damage can be done. Model Rule 3.4(e) provides that a lawyer may not allude to any matter that the lawyer does not believe is relevant and supported by admissible evidence.

---

16. MODEL RULES OF PROF'L CONDUCT, R. 1.14(b), and Comment 5.

17. RENNE, *supra* note 8.

Objection Ethics

An objection should only be made where there is a reasonable belief that the information sought is objectionable or the questioning form is improper. It is unethical to object simply as a tactic to interrupt a successful examination. Objections must have a basis, and there is no objection called "this witness is hurting my case."

Introducing Evidence

A lawyer may not allude to evidence that he does not reasonably believe is relevant or supported by admissible evidence. This rule can be interpreted to mean that a lawyer is prohibited from referring to inadmissible evidence or offering through testimony or exhibits evidence that he does not have a good-faith belief is admissible.[18] Under this analysis, introducing an exhibit that the lawyer does not believe is admissible because the opposing counsel is unskilled in objections is an ethical breach.

Lawyer as Witness

A lawyer may not be a witness in a case in which the lawyer represents a party.[19] This would seem to go without saying because of the impact it would have on the lawyer's many advocacy duties to the client, not the least of which is confidentiality. The issue arises, however, in child welfare cases where attorneys serve the dual role of attorney and guardian ad litem (GAL) for the child client. In such cases, the attorney/GAL may perform investigative duties and prepare reports. In these instances, look first to Model Rule 3.7, which prohibits the testimony as a general rule. Look next to comment 2 of Rule 3.7, which discusses the conduct of a lawyer as advocate versus fact finder. Using this analysis, one state court ruled that the determination of whether an attorney/GAL may be required to testify lies in whether the lawyer *acted* as an advocate or investigator.[20]

Candor to the Tribunal

A lawyer may not lie or introduce evidence that the lawyer knows to be false.[21] If a lawyer calls a witness—other than the client—and the witness lies, the lawyer must ask for a recess and counsel the witness to tell the truth. If the witness refuses, the lawyer must advise the court of the false testimony.

---

18. MODEL RULES OF PROF'L CONDUCT, R. 3.4(e).
19. MODEL RULES OF PROF'L CONDUCT, R. 3.7.
20. In re J.E.B., 845 P.2d 1372 (1993).
21. MODEL RULES OF PROF'L CONDUCT, R. 3.3.

If a lawyer's client lies on the stand, the lawyer must ask for a recess and advise the client to correct the lie. If the client refuses, the lawyer must move to withdraw under Model Rule 1.16. If the court denies the motion, the lawyer must reveal the lie to the court. This analysis applies presumably when a child client recants an abuse allegation and the lawyer believes the child is lying.

Witness Preparation vs. Coaching

A lawyer should prepare the witnesses. A lawyer may not "coach" a witness about what to say. Coaching occurs when the lawyer crosses the line from helping the witness communicate testimony to suggesting what the testimony should be. Ethics commentators suggest looking to the lawyer's intent in making this sometimes-difficult determination.

Ex Parte Contact

Lawyers are prohibited from ex parte contact with judges,[22] and judges are prohibited from receiving ex parte contact.[23] Attorneys should be cautious not to allow acceptable administrative contact to become substantive.

Confidentiality

A lawyer may not reveal a client confidence without the client's consent.[24] Exceptions include complying with a court order, preventing reasonably certain death or substantial bodily harm to self or others, getting advice on compliance with this rule, and preventing substantial financial injuries to others.[25]

Special confidentiality rules may exist for children's counsel. Some argue that there is no client confidentiality where the client is a child and the model is GAL best interests. The reasoning is that because the duty is to protect the child's best interests, that duty trumps confidentiality. It may also be that a lawyer is a mandatory child abuse reporter under state law, in which case it is argued that disclosure is required. This is a complex discussion on which much has been written and on which there is continued debate. Lawyers should review this research[26] and be apprised of the law in their jurisdictions.

---

22. MODEL RULES OF PROF'L CONDUCT, R. 3.5.
23. CODE OF JUDICIAL CONDUCT 3B(7).
24. MODEL RULES OF PROF'L CONDUCT, R. 1.6
25. MODEL RULES OF PROF'L CONDUCT, R. 1.6(b)(3),(4),(6).
26. *See* JEAN KOH PETERS, REPRESENTING CHILDREN IN CHILD PROTECTIVE PROCEEDINGS, ETHICAL AND PRACTICAL DIMENSIONS, 2d Ed. (Mathew Bender 2001); Renne, *supra* note 8.

A Final Word on Professionalism

The practice of law is more than a job, it is a profession. There is a higher calling in the professions—in Western civilization, the original professions were theology, medicine, and law. Those who labored at the professions did so to promote something, some good greater than themselves. This is the essence of professionalism: to labor in a manner and for an outcome consistent with a greater good. It is not hard to see a greater good in the practice of child welfare law. We work to serve children and families.

Yet the rigors and reality of day-to-day practice test our professionalism. We struggle to be courteous, respectful, honest, diligent, and humble. We are overworked. We are underpaid. Judges can be intolerant of our best efforts. Children and parents can be difficult clients. State agency bureaucracies can be rigid and short-sighted. Opposing counsel can confuse advocacy with belligerence.

It may be useful to remember that these are but the times that test our professionalism. Integrity only exists when it is challenged.

APPENDIX

Ten Trial Skills Take-Aways

1

Case Analysis: Telling the Story of the Family

Theory + Theme = Case Story + Law = Outcome

2

Direct Examination: The Words of the Story

Tell the witness's part of the story with nonleading
sensory perception questions, divided by topic and headlines.

3

Closing Argument: Story of the Case + Law = Verdict

Argue that the facts + law = verdict for your client.

Be brief and clear and show appropriate passion for your position.

4

Cross-Examination: Minimizing and Marginalizing Witness Impact

Minimize and marginalize the impact of direct with short, precise,
factual statements.

Be firm, not rude.

Be realistic and cautious.

Get your closing facts and get out.

5

Expert Witness Examination: Moving from Perception to Belief

Elicit a compelling opinion through eight phases of expert exam:

1. Introduction
2. Context
3. Accreditation
4. Tender
5. Opinion
6. Assignment
7. Basis
8. Persuasion

Cross-examine with caution as to bias and assumptions, not conclusions.

6

Difficult Witnesses: Managing the Challenge

Anticipate, avoid, remain poised, exercise control techniques, impeach, refresh, and move along.

7

Exhibits and Their Foundations: "Picture This!"

Eight Steps:

Mark, Show, Approach, Identify, Lay Foundation (HARPO[1]), Offer, Publish, Use

---

1. Hearsay, Authentic, Relevant, Personal Knowledge, Original.

8

Making and Meeting Objections: Enforcing the Rules of the Trial

Enforce and abide by the rules of trial.

Object to form and substance to support case story.

Make short, clear, recognized, and professional objections.

Make and meet objections with precision and professionalism.

Focus on the Big Three: Relevance, Foundation, and Hearsay.

9

Opening Statement: Imprinting the Story

Imprint the case story through a persuasive evidence preview.

Identify issues, explain contentions, address opposition, and ask for relief.

Do not argue.

10

Ethics and Professionalism: Integrity in the Courtroom

Lawyers are officers of the legal system, citizens with special responsibilities for the quality of justice, and representatives of clients.

Trial lawyers are all of these things in the courtroom.

INDEX

A

Adjudication
stages of a case, 4

Adoption
stages of a case, 5

Adverse witnesses, 80, 81

Answer/impeachment chart
cross-examination, 50, 51

Attorney ethics and professionalism, 133–140. *See* Ethics and professionalism

B

Battered child syndrome
expert witness testimony on syndrome evidence, 54

Bench trials
findings of fact and conclusions of law, 5
closing argument, 36
storytelling, 2

Bookending
closing argument, 35

C

Case analysis, 1–11
bench trials
findings of fact and conclusions of law, 5
storytelling, 2
CAS (case analysis summary), 8
sample form, 9
definition, 1
direct examination, 15
federal model, 3
getting started, 10, 11

GFBF (good facts/bad facts chart), 8–10
goals of a case
permanence, 3, 4
safety, 3
well-being, 4, 5
jury instructions, 5
legal framework of a case, 3–5
order of case analysis, 11
order of case preparation, 11
PC (proof chart), 10
stages of a case, 4, 5
story devices, 7, 8
story of the family, 2
theme of the case, 6, 7
theory, 5, 6
tools, 8–10
trial skills take-aways, 141

Certainty standard
expert witnesses, 56

Child sexual abuse accommodation syndrome
expert witnesses
testimony on syndrome evidence, 54

Child witness as difficult witness, 88

Closing argument, 33–39
arguments to be made, 34, 35
factual argument, 37, 38
legal argument, 38
bookending, 35
brevity, 34
don'ts, 36, 37
emotion, 36
exhibits, 35, 36
facts, promise to show, 37
factual argument, 37, 38
grabber, 37

D

Defendants
theme of the case, importance, 7

Difficult witnesses, 77–88
adverse witnesses, 80, 81
child witnesses, 88
cross-examination
agreement from witness, 78
asking judge for help, 80
attorney as authority figure, 79
deflection from witness, 79, 80
diplomacy and when to get
tough, 80
move to strike, nonresponsive, 79
pace, establishing, 79
question review, 78
re-asking the question, 79
reasoning with the witness, 80
"stop sign" or raising one's hand
to cut off witness, 80
techniques for witness control,
78–80
"your answer is . . ." technique,
79
direct examination question review,
78
good questions get good answers,
77, 78
hostile witnesses, 81
impeachment, 81–85
importance of well-conducted
impeachment, 82
omission, 84, 85
prior inconsistent statement,
82-84
lawyers quarreling with witnesses, 77
leading questions for special types of
witnesses, 87
objections
nonresponsive, 114
recorded recollection, 86, 87
refreshing recollection, 85, 86
special types of witnesses, 87, 88

child witnesses, 88
testing questions against good technique, 78
trial skills take-aways, 142

Direct examination, 13–32
accreditation of witness, 20–23
basic criteria to be met, 16
checking your work, 31, 32
case analysis, 15
defensive direct, 30
description of the action, 26–29
difficult witnesses
direct examination question
review, 78
engaging with the witness, 29, 30
expert witnesses, 56–68. *See* Expert
witnesses
failure to distinguish facts from conclusions, 15
focus on the witness, 15, 16
headlines
examples, 22–27
techniques for questioning, 19,
20
honest words
examples, 21–28
techniques for questioning, 18,
19
importance, 13
introduction of witness, 20–23
leading questions, rule against, 17,
18
loopback questions
examples, 22, 25
techniques for questioning, 20
open questions, 18
organization, 20–29
overstating witness's scope of information, 15
preparation of witness, 16, 17
ethics and professionalism, 138,
139
primacy, starting strong, 31
recency, ending strong, 31

V

Verdict
closing argument
asking for verdict, 38
opening statement
relief being sought, 131

Visual aids
closing argument, 35, 36
direct examination, 30
exhibits, 89–105. *See* Exhibits

W

Well-being
goals of a case, 4, 5

Witnesses
adverse witnesses, 80, 81
child witnesses, 88
cross-examination, 41–51. *See* Cross-examination
difficult witnesses, 77–88. *See* Difficult witnesses
direct examination, 13–32. *See* Direct examination
expert witnesses, 53–75. *See* Expert witnesses
hostile witnesses, 81
lawyer as witness, 138
recorded recollection, 86, 87
refreshing recollection, 85, 86

ABOUT THE AUTHOR

Marvin Ventrell is a lawyer, author, and teacher. He is the Executive Director of the Juvenile Law Society (JLS) headquartered in Denver, Colorado. JLS is a non-profit organization dedicated to promoting social justice for children and youth throughout the world. Mr. Ventrell began his career as a trial lawyer in Billings, Montana, in 1985. From 1985 to 1994 he tried numerous bench and jury trials each year in civil, criminal, and juvenile court. From 1990 to 1994 he served as Juvenile Public Defender for Yellowstone County, Montana. From 1994 to 2009, he served as the Chief Executive Officer of the National Association of Counsel for Children in Denver. He is an instructor for the National Institute for Trial Advocacy specialty, regional, and national programs. He has served as a consultant, lecturer and trainer for the American Bar Association, the National Council of Juvenile and Family Court Judges, The National Center for State Courts, the U.S Department of Health and Human Services Children's Bureau, the Kempe Children's Center, the International Society for the Prevention and Treatment of Child Abuse, the University of Colorado School of Medicine, and numerous law schools. He is the author of numerous articles and book chapters on trial advocacy and juvenile law, including a comprehensive history of the juvenile court published in "The Juvenile and Family Court Journal." He co-authored and edited the treatise "Child Welfare Law and Practice" as part of the national project he directed, creating the national program to certify lawyers as specialists in child welfare law. In 2004, Mr. Ventrell served as the expert witness in the federal court *Kenny A.* case, in which his testimony is cited for the holding that children have a constitutional right to the full benefit of legal counsel in child welfare cases. He is a fellow of the Colorado Bar Foundation and a recipient of the ABA National Child Advocate Award and the distinguished Kempe Award.